Collins

真正的上海数学

Real Shanghai Mathematics

6.2

Pupil Textbook

世纪出版

上海教育出版社
SHANGHAI EDUCATIONAL
PUBLISHING HOUSE

MIX
Paper from
responsible sources
FSC™ C007454

This book is produced from independently certified FSC™ paper
to ensure responsible forest management.

For more information visit: **www.harpercollins.co.uk/green**

William Collins' dream of knowledge for all began with the publication of his first book in 1819. A self-educated mill worker, he not only enriched millions of lives, but also founded a flourishing publishing house. Today, staying true to this spirit, Collins books are packed with inspiration, innovation and practical expertise. They place you at the centre of a world of possibility and give you exactly what you need to explore it.

Collins. Freedom to teach.

Collins
An imprint of HarperCollins*Publishers*
The News Building
1 London Bridge Street
London
SE1 9GF

> **Browse the complete Collins catalogue at**
> **www.collins.co.uk**

The educational materials in this book were compiled in accordance with the course curriculum produced by the Shanghai Schools (Pre-Schools) Curriculum Reform Commission and 'Maths Syllabus for Shanghai Schools (Trial Implementation)' for use in Primary 6 Second Term under the nine-year compulsory education system.

These educational materials were compiled by the head of Shanghai Normal University, and reviewed and approved for trial use by Shanghai Schools Educational Materials Review Board.

The writers for this book's educational materials are:
Editors-in-Chief: Qiu Wanzuo, Huang Hua

Guest Writers (Listed by Chinese character strokes in surname):
Zhang Yun, Ke Xinli, Xia Yingping, Xu Xiaoyan, Huang Hua

For the English edition:

Primary Publishing Director: Lee Newman
Primary Publishing Managers: Fiona McGlade, Lizzie Catford
Editorial Project Manager: Mike Appleton
Editorial Manager: Amanda Harman
Editorial Assistant: Holly Blood
Managing Translator: Huang Xingfeng
Translators: Cai Yufeng, Chen Yilin, Huang Chunhua, Ling Yujie, Xu Chengyi, Xu Huijing, Xu Yiwen, Yao Danting, Zhang Mingzhu, Zhang Yunji, Zhao Yaming, Zheng Shuting
Lead Editor: Tanya Solomons
Proofreaders: Claire Hughes, Debbie Oliver, Joan Miller
Cover artist: Amparo Barrera
Designer: Ken Vail Graphic Design
Production Controller: Sarah Burke
Printed and bound by CPI Group (UK) Ltd, Croydon, CR0 4YY

Photo acknowledgements
The publishers wish to thank the following for permission to reproduce photographs. Every effort has been made to trace copyright holders and to obtain their permission for the use of copyright materials. The publishers will gladly receive any information enabling them to rectify any error or omission at the first opportunity.

p51 dpa picture alliance/Alamy Stock Photo, p80 r.nagy/ Shutterstock, p116 normallens/Shutterstock, p137 XYZ/ Shutterstock.com

All other images with permission from Shanghai Century Publishing Group.

Contents

Unit Seven: Constructing line segments and angles   87

Unit Eight: Recognising cuboids 115

Unit Five: Rational numbers

How many metres taller is Jin Mao Tower than Park Hotel?

420 – 84

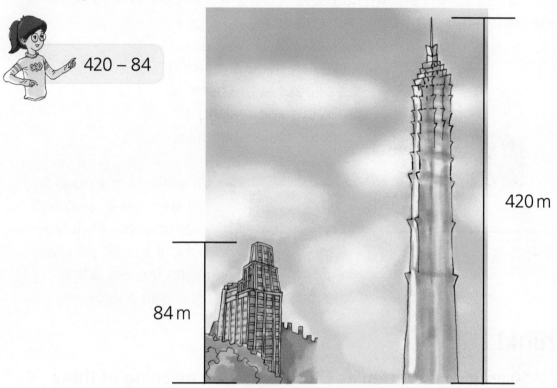

420 m

84 m

How many metres above the bottom of Huang Pu River is the deck of Yang Pu Bridge?

48 m

0 (water level)

−10 m

48 − (−10) = ?

Section One: Rational numbers
5.1 Interpreting rational numbers

In real life, we often encounter opposing ideas of quantity, such as profit and loss, income and expense, increase and decrease, and rise and fall. You have learned about negative numbers and know that positive and negative numbers can represent 'opposite' quantities.

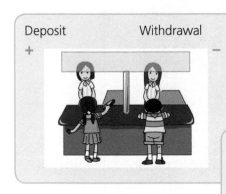

Deposit   Withdrawal
+   −

We can think of making a deposit in the bank as positive and making a withdrawal as negative.

− +

If we take the position of the tree as zero and consider the right side of the tree as positive, then the left side of the tree is negative.

 Think!

1. **If 50 pounds is written as £50, what is the meaning of these quantities?**

    a. £20   **b.** £2.50   **c.** −£80   **d.** £0

2. **If 6 degrees Celsius is written as 6 °C, how is 4 °C below zero written?**

Numbers such as 6, 2.5, $\frac{3}{4}$ or 1.2% are **positive** numbers.
Negative numbers have a minus sign in front of the numeral, such as −4, −1.2, $-\frac{3}{4}$, −2%. Sometimes, for emphasis, a plus sign will be added before a positive number, such as +6, +2.5 and $+\frac{1}{2}$. Zero is neither a positive number nor a negative number. Zero and all positive numbers can also called **non-negative** numbers. While zero and all negative numbers can be called **non-positive** numbers.

Example 1 Put the numbers in the corresponding ovals.

$$-12, 71, -2.8, \frac{1}{6}, 0, 7\frac{1}{2}, 34\%, 0.67, -\frac{3}{4}, \frac{12}{7}, -\frac{9}{5}$$

Solution

$$71, \frac{1}{6}, 7\frac{1}{2}, 34\%, 0.67, \frac{12}{7}$$

$$-12, -2.8, -\frac{3}{4}, -\frac{9}{5}$$

positive numbers   negative numbers

 # Think!

Zero is the boundary between positive and negative numbers. →

Should zero be put in either of the two ovals?

71 is a positive number, −5 is a negative number and 0 is neither. They are all integers.

$\frac{1}{6}$, $7\frac{1}{2}$ and $\frac{12}{7}$ are positive fractions while $-\frac{3}{4}$ and $-\frac{9}{5}$ are negative fractions.

They are all fractions.
Fractions can be positive or negative.

Integers and fractions are collectively called **rational numbers**.

- Rational numbers
  - Integers
    - Positive integers
    - Zero
    - Negative integers
  - Fractions
    - Positive fractions
    - Negative fractions

 You can think of an integer as a fraction with denominator 1. In this sense, all rational numbers are fractions.

Example 2 Which of these numbers are integers? Which are positive numbers? Which are negative numbers? And which are rational numbers?

$$8, -3, 7\frac{1}{2}, -\frac{1}{6}, 69, 0, 0.32, -1\frac{2}{5}, -3.1$$

Solution 8, –3, 69 and 0 are integers.

8, $7\frac{1}{2}$, 69 and 0.32 are positive numbers.

–3, $-\frac{1}{6}$, $-1\frac{2}{5}$ and –3.1 are negative numbers.

8, –3, $7\frac{1}{2}$, $-\frac{1}{6}$, 69, 0, 0.32, $-1\frac{2}{5}$ and –3.1 are all rational numbers.

Because there are different types of calculator, the way your calculator works may be different from the method shown here. If this method does not work on your calculator, refer to its instruction manual.

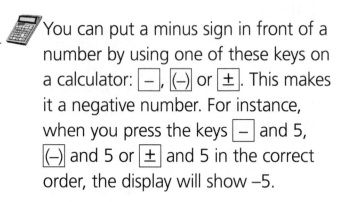 You can put a minus sign in front of a number by using one of these keys on a calculator: $\boxed{-}$, $\boxed{(-)}$ or $\boxed{\pm}$. This makes it a negative number. For instance, when you press the keys $\boxed{-}$ and 5, $\boxed{(-)}$ and 5 or $\boxed{\pm}$ and 5 in the correct order, the display will show –5.

Practice 5.1

1. a. Among the numbers –2, 25, 0, $\frac{3}{5}$, –0.35 and $-\frac{1}{3}$, the positive numbers are _____ and the negative numbers are _____.

   b. If we take east as positive in direction, what is meant by –50 metres? If we now take south as positive in direction, what is meant by –50 metres?

2. Think of 6 positive numbers and 6 negative numbers and write them in the correct brackets.

Positive numbers: {   }   Negative numbers: {   }

3. Are these numbers positive, negative or non-negative? Put each number in the correct oval(s).

$-15, 5\frac{1}{3}, -0.23, 0.51, 0, -0.65, 7.6, 2, -\frac{3}{5}, 1.5\%.$

positive numbers   negative numbers   non-negative numbers

5.2 Number lines

Do you remember how to construct a number line, and how to use the points on a number line to represent rational numbers?

You know that a **number line** defines the origin, and has direction and sections of unit length.

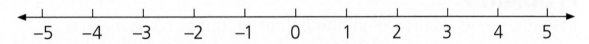

2 is represented by the point on this number line that is 2 units to the right of the origin.

3.4 is represented by the point on this number line that is 3.4 units to the right of the origin.

−3 is represented by the point on this number line that is 3 units to the left of the origin.

$-\frac{1}{2}$ is represented by the point on this number line that is $\frac{1}{2}$ of a unit to the left of the origin.

> Any rational number can be represented by a point on a number line.

Example 1   Which numbers are represented by the points A, B, C, D and E on this number line?

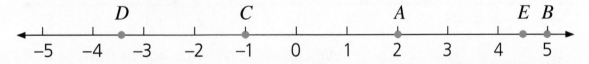

The points can represent both decimals and fractions. $\longrightarrow$

Solution   Point A represents 2, point B represents 5, point C represents −1, point D represents $-3\frac{1}{2}$ and point E represents 4.5.

? Problem 1

What are the similarities and differences between the numbers in these three groups: 3 and −3; 4 and −4; $\frac{1}{2}$ and $-\frac{1}{2}$?

If two numbers are the same size but have different signs, we can say one is the **opposite** of the other. We say that the two numbers are **opposite numbers**. The opposite of zero is zero.

The opposite of $2\frac{1}{3}$ is $-2\frac{1}{3}$, the opposite of $-2\frac{1}{3}$ is $2\frac{1}{3}$, and $2\frac{1}{3}$ and $-2\frac{1}{3}$ are opposite numbers.

? Problem 2

Mark the points that represent these three groups of numbers on a number line: 3 and -3, 4 and -4, and $\frac{1}{2}$ and $-\frac{1}{2}$. What do you notice?

On the number line, two points that represent opposite numbers are on different sides of the origin and are at an equal distance from the origin.

The points that represent 3 and -3 on the number line are on different sides of the origin and they are at an equal distance from the origin.

Example 2 Mark the points on the number line that represent 3, 5, $-2\frac{1}{2}$, 1.2 and their respective opposite numbers.

Solution The opposite of -3 is 3, the opposite of 5 is -5, the opposite of $-2\frac{1}{2}$ is $2\frac{1}{2}$ and the opposite of 1.2 is -1.2. They are shown on the number line as follows:

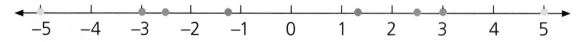

The opposite of a negative number is the positive number it corresponds to.

$\longrightarrow$

We can write a minus sign in front of a number to represent its opposite number. For instance, the opposite of 3 is -3 and the opposite of -3 is $-(-3) = 3$. The opposite of a number's opposite number is the original number itself. So the opposite of 3's opposite number is still 3.

Notice that putting a minus sign in front of a negative number changes it to a positive number.

Practice 5.2

1. Put each number in the correct oval(s).

$$-5, 3.7, 0, 300, -1.01, 889, -4\frac{3}{7}, \frac{12}{11}$$

integers   negative rational   non-negative numbers
                   numbers

2. Mark the points that represent 3.5, $\frac{1}{3}$, $-2\frac{1}{4}$, 0 and their respective opposite numbers on the number line.

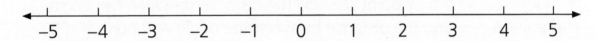

3. Which of these numbers are equal? Which numbers are opposites?

$$2.3, -5, -1\frac{1}{2}, 2\frac{3}{10}, 4.5, 5, 1\frac{1}{2}, -3.2$$

4. Which of these statements is/are correct?

A. Positive numbers and negative numbers are opposite numbers.

B. Two numbers that represent opposite quantities are opposite numbers.

C. Every rational number has an opposite number.

D. The opposite number of any number is a negative number.

5.3 Absolute value

💡 Think!

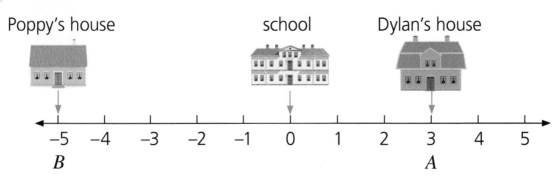

Poppy's house   school   Dylan's house

How far away is Poppy's house from the school? How far away is Dylan's house from the school? (Each unit on the number line represents 1 km.)

On the number line, the number represented by point A is 3 and the number represented by point B is –5. The distance between the origin and point A is 3, and the distance between the origin and point B is 5. 3 is the absolute value of 3, and 5 is the absolute value of –5.

> The distance between a number's position on the number line and the origin is called the **absolute value** of the number.

We use the symbol $|a|$ to represent the absolute value of the number a. For example:

The absolute value of 4 is 4, which is written as: $|4| = 4$

The absolute value of –3 is 3, which is written as: $|-3| = 3$

The absolute value of 0 is 0, which is written as: $|0| = 0$

Example 1   Find the absolute values of 3.7, –12, 0 and $-3\frac{1}{2}$.

Solution $|3.7| = 3.7$ $|-12| = 12$ $|0| = 0$ $|-3\frac{1}{2}| = 3\frac{1}{2}$

📝 Summary

$|3\frac{1}{2}| = 3\frac{1}{2}$

$|-2.1| = 2.1$

$|0| = 0$

⟶ The absolute value of a positive number is itself.
The absolute value of a negative number is its opposite number.
The absolute value of zero is zero.

Think!

1. What does the absolute value of a number mean in relation to the number line?

2. What is the relationship between the absolute values of two numbers that are opposite numbers?

 # Observation

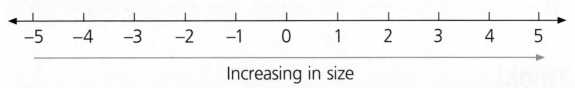

Increasing in size

Every rational number can be represented as a single point on a number line. This means that any two rational numbers can be compared easily on a number line because the number on the right is always greater than the number on the left. For example, $5 > 0$, $0 > -4$ and $5 > -4$.

> Positive numbers are greater than zero. Zero is greater than negative numbers. Positive numbers are greater than negative numbers.

The greater the distance between the position of a number on the number line and the origin (0), the greater the absolute value of that number. The smaller the distance between the position of a number on the number line and the origin (0), the smaller the absolute value of that number.

Example 2 Show these numbers on a number line and arrange them from smallest to greatest.

$5, 0, -1\frac{1}{2}, 4.5, -1$

Solution Mark the points for the numbers on the number line.

From the number line we can see that their order from smallest to greatest is:

$-1\frac{1}{2}, -1, 0, 4.5, 5$

So: $-1\frac{1}{2} < -1 < 0 < 4.5 < 5$

Example 3 Compare -3.5 and $-2\frac{3}{5}$.

Solution Mark the points representing -3.5 and $-2\frac{3}{5}$ on a number line:

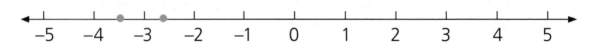

We can see from the number line that the point that represents $-2\frac{3}{5}$ is to the right of the point that represents -3.5, so $-2\frac{3}{5} > -3.5$.

Think!

How can we compare $|-3.5|$ and $|-2\frac{3}{5}|$?

$|-3.5| = 3.5,\ |-2\frac{3}{5}| = 2\frac{3}{5}.$ $\qquad$ $3.5 > 2\frac{3}{5}$, so $|-3.5| > |-2\frac{3}{5}|.$

> When we compare two negative numbers, the number with a greater absolute value is actually the smaller one.

Practice 5.3

What can you conclude?

1. **a.** On a number line, the rational number represented by the point that is 3.5 units from the origin is _____.

   b. The absolute value of _____ is itself, and the absolute value of _____ is its opposite number.

2. **Write the integers with absolute values less than 5 and show them on a number line.**

3. **When a is a rational number, can $-a$ be a negative number?**

4. **Use > or < to compare these numbers.**

   -7 _____ -5 $\qquad$ $-|-2|$ _____ $-(-2)$ $\qquad$ -0.125 _____ $-|\frac{1}{4}|$

5. **Use > or < to compare these numbers.**

   a. -437 and 0 $\qquad$ **b.** $-\frac{26}{137}$ and 0 $\qquad$ **c.** 0.3% and -17

   d. -16.3 and -16.4 $\qquad$ **e.** $\frac{13}{27}$ and $\frac{30}{59}$ $\qquad$ **f.** $-\frac{17}{50}$ and -0.32

Section Two: Operations with rational numbers

5.4 Adding rational numbers

You have learned about addition in relation to positive integers and zero. Introducing negative numbers means expanding its application from integers to rational numbers. How do we add rational numbers?

> A profit means that the shop takes in more money than it spends. A loss is the opposite.

 Think!

If we decide that profit is 'positive', then loss must be 'negative'. Look at the profits and losses for a business in Dublin, over a period of four years.

Year 1: the first half-year profit is 1.2 million euros and the second half-year profit is 0.8 million euros.

Year 2: the first half-year profit is −0.6 million euros and the second half-year profit is 0.7 million euros.

> Making a profit of −0.6 million euros means the same as making a loss of 0.6 million euros.

Year 3: the first half-year profit is −0.5 million euros and the second half-year profit is 0.5 million euros.

Year 4: the first half-year profit is 0.9 million euros and the second half-year profit is −0.1 million euros.

Does this business make a profit or a loss each year? What is its profit or loss?

Complete the table showing the profit and loss of the business throughout the four years.

	Calculation	Solution (million euros)
First year	1.2 + 0.8	
Second year	(−0.6) + (−0.7)	−1.3
Third year	(−0.5) + 0.5	
Fourth year	0.9 + (−0.1)	

Summary

Rules for the addition of rational numbers

To add two numbers with the same (plus or minus) sign, add their absolute values. The sign of the result is the same as the sign shared by the two numbers.

When two numbers with different signs are added, if their absolute values are the same, the result is zero. If not, the absolute value of the result is the difference between the two numbers' absolute values, and the sign is the same as that of the number with the greater absolute value.

When we add a number to zero, the result is the number itself.

Example 1 Add these rational numbers.

   a. $(-12) + (-36)$ **b.** $\left(-\dfrac{2}{3}\right) + \left(-\dfrac{1}{3}\right)$ ←—————— Add two numbers with the same sign.

   c. $\left(-1\dfrac{1}{4}\right) + 0$

Solution

   a. $(-12) + (-36) = -(12 + 36) = -48$

   b. $\left(-\dfrac{2}{3}\right) + \left(-\dfrac{1}{3}\right) = -\left(\dfrac{2}{3} + \dfrac{1}{3}\right) = -1$

   c. $\left(-1\dfrac{1}{4}\right) + 0 = -1\dfrac{1}{4}$ ←—— Add a number to zero.

Example 2 Add these rational numbers.

   a. $3 + (-3)$ **b.** $(-16) + 5$ ←—————— Add two numbers with different signs.

   c. $\dfrac{11}{25} + (-2)$ **d.** $24 + (-5.5)$

Solution

   a. $3 + (-3) = 0$

$|-16| > |5|$

   b. $(-16) + 5 = -(16 - 5) = -11$ ←———————— $(-11) + (-5) + 5 = -11$

   c. $\dfrac{11}{25} + (-2) = -\left(2 - \dfrac{11}{25}\right) = -\left(\dfrac{50}{25} - \dfrac{11}{25}\right)$

$$= -\dfrac{39}{25} = -1\dfrac{14}{25}$$

   d. $24 + (-5.5) = 24 - 5.5 = 18.5$

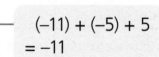

Example 3   A truck that carries goods starts from station A. First, it travels east for 15 km and unloads. Then it travels west for 25 km and is loaded with other goods. Finally, it travels east again for 20 km. Where does the truck finally stop?

Solution   West to east is set as the positive direction.

15 + (−25) + 20

= (−10) + 20 = 10 (km)

So the truck finally stops 10 kilometres to the east of station A.

Draw a route chart representing the calculation above.

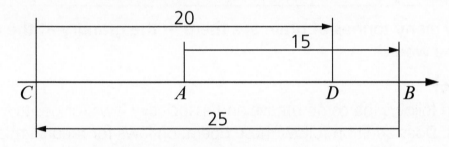

As shown, the three trips made by the truck are from A to B, from B to C and from C to D, so point D is the final position of the truck.

Practice 5.4 (1)

1. Write the answers to these sums.

a. $\left(-\dfrac{1}{2}\right) + \left(-\dfrac{1}{3}\right)$ b. $\dfrac{1}{2} + \dfrac{1}{3}$ c. $(-0.1) + -\dfrac{2}{3}$

d. $(-4) + \left(-\dfrac{2}{5}\right)$ e. $\left(-\dfrac{5}{26}\right) + 0$ f. $(-3) + (-9) + \left(-\dfrac{2}{7}\right)$

2. Emma had £450 in her account. She first withdrew £80 and then withdrew £150. How much money is there in her account now?

3. One night, the temperature was −1 °C at 19:00. The temperature had dropped by 3 degrees at 23:30. What was the temperature at that time?

4. Write the answers to these sums.

a. $7 + (-5)$ b. $\left(-\dfrac{3}{4}\right) + \dfrac{1}{2}$ c. $\dfrac{5}{6} + \left(-\dfrac{4}{7}\right)$ d. $3.4 + (-7.2)$

5. The original altitude of a plane was 8000 metres. It rose by 300 metres and then it dropped by 200 metres. At what altitude is the plane flying now?

6. On Monday morning there were 200 tonnes of grain in a granary. The table shows information about purchases and sales of grain over the week.

	Monday	Tuesday	Wednesday	Thursday	Friday
Purchases (tonnes)	50	30	60	40	50
Sales (tonnes)	−30	−40	−50	−40	−10

How many tonnes of grain are there in the granary at the end of the week?

 ## Think!

Addition follows the commutative and associative laws for positive integers. Does addition follow these operation laws for rational numbers?

Work out the answers to these calculations.

    a. $(-3) + 8.1 = ?$ $8.1 + (-3) = ?$

    b. $[5.3 + (-3.4)] + 2 = ?$ $5.3 + [(-3.4) + 2] = ?$

 Write down some similar sets of questions to those above. Use a calculator to work out the answers. What is the rule?

 ## Summary

When we add two rational numbers, the sum remains the same even if we swap the two addends.

When we add three rational numbers, the sum remains the same whether we add the first two numbers and then add the third, or add the second and third numbers and then add the first.

Rules for the addition of rational numbers

Commutative law: $a + b = b + a$ Associative law: $(a + b) + c = a + (b + c)$

Looking at the commutative and associative laws of addition, we can see that when adding rational numbers, we can swap the addends and add them in any order, and/or add some of them separately to start with.

Example 4 Add these rational numbers.

a. $16 + (-25) + 24 + (-32)$ **b.** $0.125 + 2\frac{1}{4} + \left(-2\frac{1}{8}\right) + (-0.25)$

Solution

a. $16 + (-25) + 24 + (-32)$

$= (16 + 24) + (-25) + (-32)$ (**Commutative law of addition**)

$= (16 + 24) + [(-25) + (-32)]$ (**Associative law of addition**)

$= 40 + (-57)$

$= -17$ ⟵ First add the two pairs of numbers that have the same sign.

b. $0.125 + 2\frac{1}{4} + \left(-2\frac{1}{8}\right) + (-0.25)$

$= 0.125 + \left(-2\frac{1}{8}\right) + 2\frac{1}{4} + (-0.25)$ (**Commutative law of addition**)

$= [0.125 + \left(-2\frac{1}{8}\right)] + [2\frac{1}{4} + (-0.25)]$ (**Associative law of addition**)

$= (-2) + 2$

$= 0$ ⟵ $\dfrac{1}{8} = 0.125$

$\dfrac{1}{4} = 0.25$

Practice 5.4 (2)

1. Add these rational numbers.

   a. $23 + (-17) + 16 + (-22)$ **b.** $(-12) + 23 + 11 + (-3) + 5 + (-4)$

   c. $(-7) + (-6.5) + (-3) + 6.5$ **d.** $(-9) + 5\frac{3}{4} + 9 + \left(-5\frac{3}{4}\right)$

   e. $1 + \left(-\frac{1}{2}\right) + \frac{1}{3} + \left(-\frac{1}{6}\right)$

2. Add these rational numbers.

   a. $(-8.2) + 10 + 2 + (-1.8)$

   b. $(-0.8) + (-0.7) + (-2.1) + 0.8 + 3.5$

   c. $\frac{1}{4} + \left(-\frac{2}{3}\right) + \frac{4}{5} + \left(-\frac{1}{4}\right) + \left(-\frac{1}{3}\right)$

   d. $(-0.5) + 3\frac{1}{4} + 2.75 + \left(-5\frac{1}{2}\right)$

15

5.5 Subtracting rational numbers

💡 Think!

The table below shows the temperature in Shanghai on two days in winter.

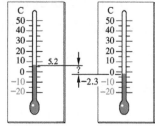

	Maximum temperature (°C)	Minimum temperature (°C)
First day	9.1	2.3
Second day	5.2	−2.3

On which of the two days is the temperature difference greater?

This is a problem involving the subtraction of rational numbers. The relevant equations are:

$9.1 - 2.3$ and $5.2 - (-2.3)$

$9.1 - 2.3 = 6.8$, but how do we find $5.2 - (-2.3)$?

Subtraction is the inverse operation of addition.

$5.2 - (-2.3) = 5.2 + 2.3$

subtracting a negative is the
same as adding a positive

$5.2 + 2.3 = 7.5$

So $5.2 - (-2.3) = 7.5$

$7.5 + (-2.3) = 5.2$ ◄——— We made the equation $5.2 - (-2.3) = a$. From this we found a value for a that made the equation $a + (-2.3) = 5.2$ true.

The temperature difference on the first day is 6.8 degrees, and the temperature difference on the second day is 7.5 degrees. So the temperature difference on the second day is greater than on the first day.

📝 Summary

> **Rule for the subtraction of rational numbers**
> Subtracting a number is equivalent to adding the opposite of that number. $a - b = a + (-b)$.

Example 1 Subtract these rational numbers.

a. $6 - (-6)$ **b.** $0 - 9$ **c.** $\left(-5\frac{1}{2}\right) - \left(-3\frac{1}{4}\right)$ **d.** $\left(-1\frac{1}{2}\right) - \frac{1}{3}$

Solution

a. $6 - (-6) = 6 + 6 = 12$ ← Subtracting −6 is equivalent to adding 6.

b. $0 - 9 = 0 + (-9) = -9$

c. $\left(-5\frac{1}{2}\right) - \left(-3\frac{1}{4}\right) = \left(-5\frac{1}{2}\right) + 3\frac{1}{4} = -2\frac{1}{4}$ ← Subtracting $-3\frac{1}{4}$ is equivalent to adding $3\frac{1}{4}$.

d. $\left(-1\frac{1}{2}\right) - \frac{1}{3} = \left(-1\frac{1}{2}\right) + \left(-\frac{1}{3}\right) = -1\frac{5}{6}$

Example 2 A bridge crosses a river. The distance between the deck of the bridge and the surface of the river is about 48 metres. The distance between the bottom of the river and the surface of the river is about 10 metres. What is the approximate distance (in metres) between the deck of the bridge and the river bottom?

Solution If we can say the direction from the river to the sky is the positive direction, then $48 - (-10) = 48 + 10 = 58$ (metres).

So the distance between the deck of the bridge and the bottom of the river is about 58 metres.

Practice 5.5

1. Complete these subtractions in your head and say the answers aloud.

   a. $10 - (-7)$ **b.** $8 - (-10)$ **c.** $0 - (-3)$

   d. $(-11) - 10$ **e.** $(-6) - (-9)$ **f.** $(-47) - 12$

   g. $0.5 - (-0.5)$ **h.** $26 - 13$ **i.** $(-33) - 22$

2. Subtract these rational numbers.

   a. $7\frac{2}{3} - 3\frac{1}{6}$ **b.** $\left(-4\frac{1}{7}\right) - \left(-5\frac{6}{7}\right)$

   c. $3\frac{1}{4} - (-4.25)$ **d.** $(-0.8) - 1\frac{3}{5}$

   e. $7 + \left(-\frac{4}{7}\right) - \left(-\frac{3}{7}\right) - \left(-\frac{1}{7}\right)$ **f.** $0.8 - (-0.8)$

3. a. Which number must you add to $-5\frac{3}{4}$ to get 6?

   b. Which number gives −0.8 when −7.8 is subtracted from it?

   c. Which number gives −4 when −3.5 is subtracted from it?

   d. Which number gives $-\frac{3}{2}$ when −45 is added to it?

5.6 Multiplying rational numbers

Think!

$2 \times 1 = ?$ $\qquad$ $(-2) \times 1 = ?$ $\qquad$ $2 \times (-1) = ?$ $\qquad$ $(-2) \times (-1) = ?$

$2 \times 1 = 2$, $\quad (-2) \times 1 = -2$
Multiplying a number by 1 gives the number itself.

$2 \times (-1) = (-1) + (-1) = -2$
Multiplying a positive number by (-1) gives its opposite number.

$(-2) \times (-1) = ?$
Going one step further: $(-4) \times 3 = ?$
$(-4) \times (-3) = ?$

Look again at Poppy's answer, above. So $(-2) \times (-1)$ gives 2! Multiplying by a negative number changes the sign.

Think!

A car is moving in an east–west direction with an average speed of 80 kilometres per hour, and it is at point A now.

A

1. **If the car goes east for 2 hours, which direction will it be from point A? What will the distance be between the car and point A?**

2. **If the car goes west for 2 hours, which direction will it be from point A? What will the distance be between the car and point A?**

3. **If the car had been travelling east when it reached point A, which direction was it from point A two hours ago? What was the distance between the car and point A?**

4. **If the car had been travelling west when it reached point A, which direction was it from point A two hours ago? What was the distance between the car and point A?**

Let's call east the positive direction, which makes west the negative direction. Let's call 'after several hours' positive, which makes 'several hours ago' negative.

1. 2 × 80 = 160
After 2 hours, the car will be to the east of point A and its distance from A will be 160 kilometres.

2. 2 × (−80) = −160
After 2 hours, the car will be to the west of point A and its distance from A will be 160 kilometres.

3. (−2) × 80 = −160
2 hours ago, the car was to the west of point A and its distance from A was 160 kilometres.

4. (− 2) × (−80) = 160
2 hours ago, the car was to the east of point A and its distance from A was 160 kilometres.

Observe the plus or minus signs of the two factors and the product in the equations above. What can you conclude?

We can think of the road as a straight line. Let's view point A as the origin, the direction from west to east as the positive direction, 1 kilometre as the unit length and construct a number line accordingly.

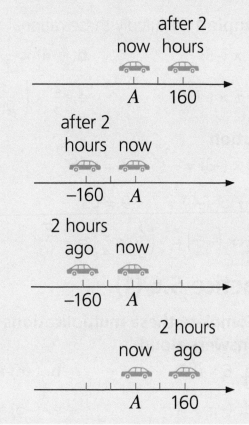

Rules for plus and minus signs when multiplying two numbers
The product of two positive numbers is positive. The product of a negative number and a positive number is negative. The product of two negative numbers is positive.

 **Think!**

0 × 80 = ?   (−80) × 0 = ?   0 × 0 = ?

(−3) × 2 = ?   (−3) × 1 = ?   (−3) × 0 = ?
(−3) × (−1) = ?   (−3) × (−2) = ?

Can you explain the examples above?

> ### Rules for the multiplication of rational numbers
> When multiplying two numbers, if they both have the same (plus or minus) sign, the sign of the product is positive. If they have different signs, the sign of the product is negative. The absolute value of the product is the product of their absolute values.
> If we multiply any number by zero, the product is zero.

Example 1 Multiply these rational numbers.

a. $5 \times (-3)$ **b.** $(-4) \times \dfrac{1}{2}$ **c.** $(-7) \times (-9)$

d. $0.5 \times (-0.6)$ **e.** $\dfrac{2}{5} \times \left(-\dfrac{3}{4}\right)$

Solution

a. $5 \times (-3) = -(5 \times 3) = -15$ **b.** $(-4) \times \dfrac{1}{2} = -\left(4 \times \dfrac{1}{2}\right) = -2$

c. $(-7) \times (-9) = 7 \times 9 = 63$ **d.** $0.5 \times (-0.6) = -(0.5 \times 0.6) = -0.3$

e. $\dfrac{2}{5} \times \left(-\dfrac{3}{4}\right) = -\left(\dfrac{2}{5} \times \dfrac{3}{4}\right) = -\dfrac{3}{10}$

Practice 5.6 (1)

1. **Complete these multiplications in your head and say the answers aloud.**

   a. $6 \times (-9)$ **b.** $(-6) \times (-9)$ **c.** $(-6) \times 9$

   d. $(-6) \times 1$ **e.** $(-6) \times (-1)$ **f.** $6 \times (-1)$

   g. $(-6) \times 0$ **h.** $0 \times (-6)$ **i.** $(-6) \times 0.25$

   j. $(0.5) \times (-8)$ **k.** $\dfrac{4}{9} \times \left(-\dfrac{3}{2}\right)$ **l.** $\left(-\dfrac{1}{3}\right) \times \dfrac{1}{4}$

2. **Multiply these rational numbers.**

   a. $(-8) \times 0.25$ **b.** $(-0.5) \times (-8)$ **c.** $\dfrac{2}{3} \times \left(-\dfrac{9}{4}\right)$

   d. $2.9 \times (-0.4)$ **e.** $(-0.3) \times \left(-\dfrac{10}{7}\right)$ **f.** $\left(-\dfrac{34}{15}\right) \times 25$

3. **Multiply these rational numbers.**

   a. $\left(-\dfrac{2}{3}\right) \times \dfrac{1}{4}$ **b.** $\left(-\dfrac{5}{6}\right) \times \left(-\dfrac{3}{10}\right)$ **c.** $1\dfrac{1}{6} \times (-0.8)$

   d. $\left(-2\dfrac{7}{13}\right) \times (-8)$ **e.** $(-0.3) \times \left(-1\dfrac{3}{7}\right)$

4. 'When multiplying two rational numbers, if we replace a factor with its opposite number, the product is the opposite number of the original product.' Is this statement correct?

5. Complete these calculations and write the answers. Can you find a rule for the plus and minus signs of the products?

a. $(-2) \times 3 \times 4 \times 5$

b. $(-2) \times (-3) \times 4 \times 5$

c. $(-2) \times (-3) \times (-4) \times 5$

d. $(-2) \times (-3) \times (-4) \times (-5)$

e. $(-2) \times (-3) \times (-4) \times (-5) \times 0$

If only one of the factors in a multiplication has a minus sign, the product is negative. If both factors in a multiplication have minus signs, their product is positive. If there are three factors with minus signs, their product is negative. If there are four factors with minus signs, their product is positive. If one of the factors is zero, the product is zero.

 Use a calculator to check whether the product is positive or negative when there are five, six, seven or more negative factors.

When multiplying several numbers that are not equal to zero, the sign of the product is determined by the number of negative factors. If the number of negative factors is an odd number, the product is negative; if the number of negative factors is an even number, the product is positive. When multiplying several numbers, if one of the factors is zero, the product is zero.

The commutative law of multiplication: $ab = ba$
The associative law of multiplication: $(ab)c = a(bc)$
The distributive law of multiplication for addition: $a(b + c) = ab + ac$

Earlier in Year 6, you used a calculator to check some operational rules for the multiplication of fractions. Do you remember those operational rules? They are still true for rational numbers. Try using a calculator to check them.

Example 2 Multiply these rational numbers:

$$\left(-1\frac{1}{2}\right) \times \left(-2\frac{1}{3}\right) \times \left(-3\frac{1}{4}\right) \times 24$$

> We can find the (plus or minus) sign of the product even before we do a calculation. We can also turn the mixed numbers into improper fractions.

Solution $\left(-1\frac{1}{2}\right) \times \left(-2\frac{1}{3}\right) \times \left(-3\frac{1}{4}\right) \times 24$

$$= -\left(\frac{3}{2} \times \frac{7}{3} \times \frac{13}{4} \times 24\right)$$

$$= -273$$

Example 3 Multiply these rational numbers: $(-12.5) \times 0.19 \times (-8)$

Solution $(-12.5) \times 0.19 \times (-8)$

$$= [(-12.5) \times (-8)] \times 0.19$$

> Use the commutative and associative laws of multiplication.

$$= 100 \times 0.19$$

$$= 19$$

Example 4 Multiply these rational numbers: $0.12 \times \left(\frac{3}{4} - \frac{1}{6}\right)$

Solution 1 $0.12 \times \left(\frac{3}{4} - \frac{1}{6}\right)$

$$= 0.12 \times \left(\frac{9}{12} - \frac{2}{12}\right)$$

$$= 0.12 \times \frac{7}{12}$$

$$= 0.07$$

Solution 2 $0.12 \times \left(\frac{3}{4} - \frac{1}{6}\right)$

$$= 0.12 \times \frac{3}{4} - 0.12 \times \frac{1}{6}$$

$$= 0.09 - 0.02$$

$$= 0.07$$

Practice 5.6 (2)

1. Multiply these rational numbers.

a. $\left(-2\frac{1}{2}\right) \times \left(-3\frac{1}{3}\right) \times (-6)$

b. $0.24 \times 1\frac{1}{6} \times \left(-\frac{5}{14}\right)$

c. $\left(-4\frac{1}{3}\right) \times \left(-1\frac{1}{2}\right) \times \frac{3}{4}$

2. Multiply these rational numbers. Use a shortcut method.

a. $(-21) \times \left(1 + \frac{1}{3} - \frac{1}{21}\right)$

b. $\left(\frac{7}{9} - \frac{11}{12}\right) \times 72 \times \left(-\frac{1}{10}\right)$

c. $(-5.35) \times (-3) + 5.35 \times (-7) + 5.35 \times 4$

d. $5.6 \times \frac{3}{8} \times \left(-\frac{1}{7}\right)$

5.7 Dividing rational numbers

Think!

How can you find $6 \div (-2)$?

$(-2) \times (-3) = 6$, so $6 \div (-2) = -3$

> Division is the inverse operation of multiplication.

Can you write the correct answers in the boxes?

$(-8) \div 4 = \square$ $\qquad$ $(-12) \div (-3) = \square$ $\qquad$ $0 \div (-2) = \square$

Looking at the formula above, what is the connection between the (plus and minus) signs of the divisor, the dividend and the quotient?

> ### Rules for the division of rational numbers
>
> When one number is divided by another, the result is positive if they have the same sign, otherwise the result will be negative. The size of the quotient is the same as the quotient of their absolute values.
>
> Dividing zero by any non-zero number always gives a result of zero.

Example 1 Divide these rational numbers.

a. $35 \div (-7)$ $\qquad\qquad$ **b.** $(-36) \div (-72)$

Solution

a. $35 \div (-7) = -(35 \div 7) = -5$ $\qquad$ **b.** $(-36) \div (-72) = \dfrac{36}{72} = \dfrac{1}{2}$

Example 2 Find the reciprocal of $-\dfrac{3}{4}$.

Solution

$1 \div \left(-\dfrac{3}{4}\right) = -\left(1 \div \dfrac{3}{4}\right) = -\left(1 \times \dfrac{4}{3}\right) = -\dfrac{4}{3}$ $\qquad$ So the reciprocal of $-\dfrac{3}{4}$ is $-\dfrac{4}{3}$

> The reciprocal of $-a$ is $-\dfrac{1}{a}$ ($a \neq 0$), and the reciprocal of $-\dfrac{p}{q}$ is $-\dfrac{q}{p}$ ($p \neq 0$, $q \neq 0$).

Example 3 Complete these calculations.

a. $(-3) \times \left(-\dfrac{3}{2}\right)$ $\qquad\qquad$ **b.** $(-3) \div \left(-\dfrac{2}{3}\right)$

Solution

a. $(-3) \times \left(-\dfrac{3}{2}\right) = 3 \times \dfrac{3}{2} = \dfrac{9}{2} = 4\dfrac{1}{2}$

b. $(-3) \div \left(-\dfrac{2}{3}\right) = 3 \div \dfrac{2}{3} = 3 \times \dfrac{3}{2} = 4\dfrac{1}{2}$

Can you find any rules for these operations?

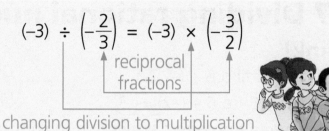

$$(-3) \div \left(-\frac{2}{3}\right) = (-3) \times \left(-\frac{3}{2}\right)$$

reciprocal fractions

changing division to multiplication

> A divided by B ($A \neq 0$, $B \neq 0$) equals A multiplied by the reciprocal of B.

Practice 5.7

1. Divide these rational numbers.

   a. $(-36) \div 4$ **b.** $42 \div (-35)$ **c.** $0 \div (-321)$

   d. $\frac{1}{2} \div (-2)$ **e.** $(-4) \div \frac{2}{3}$ **f.** $(-5) \div \left(-\frac{10}{11}\right)$

2. Find the reciprocal of each number.

   -14, $-\frac{7}{14}$, -0.25, -1, 1

3. Workers in a factory are expected to complete a target number of products every day. If they produce more than the target number, this is called overproduction. The table shows the daily overproduction for two workers (A and B) over 10 days. (units: cases)

Day	1	2	3	4	5	6	7	8	9	10
A	7	6	-2	0	5	-3	4	6	5	8
B	5	2	-6	2	-3	-4	-7	0	-4	-8

   a. What do the positive and negative numbers in this table mean?

   b. Workers are rewarded if their daily overproduction is more than 2 cases on average. Are A and B entitled to a reward for these 10 days of work?

5.8 Powers of rational numbers

Try it out!

If a sheet of paper can be divided into 2 parts when it is folded once, and into 4 parts when folded twice, how many parts will you get if you fold the sheet 3 times?

Think!

If you could fold the sheet of paper 5 times, 10 times or 20 times, how many parts would you get? How will you write the answer?

The number sentence for multiplying 2 by 2 twenty times in a row is far too long. Is there a shorter way to write it?

You can write it as: $2 \times 2 \times 2 \times 2 \times 2$,

$\underbrace{2 \times 2 \times 2 \times \ldots \times 2 \times 2}_{\text{10 \textbf{groups of} 2}}$ $\underbrace{2 \times 2 \times 2 \times \ldots \times 2 \times 2}_{\text{20 \textbf{groups of} 2}}$

Do you remember what 2^2 and 2^3 mean?

Generally, the operation when n 'lots' of the same factor a are multiplied together, is written as a^n.

base number → a^n ← exponent

power

A product made up of the same factor multiplied by itself is called a **power**. For example, 'a' is the **base number** of an and 'n' is its **exponent**. an is read as 'a to the power of n'.

$1^n = 1$ and $0^n = 0$
(where n is a positive integer).

$$\underbrace{2 \times 2 \times \ldots \times 2 \times 2}_{\text{20 groups of 2}} = 2^{20}$$

Example 1 What number does each of these represent?

a. 10^5 **b.** $(-3)^4$ **c.** $\left(-\dfrac{1}{2}\right)^3$

Solution

a. $10^5 = 10 \times 10 \times 10 \times 10 \times 10 = 100\,000$

b. $(-3)^4 = (-3) \times (-3) \times (-3) \times (-3) = 81$

c. $\left(-\dfrac{1}{2}\right)^3 = \left(-\dfrac{1}{2}\right) \times \left(-\dfrac{1}{2}\right) \times \left(-\dfrac{1}{2}\right) = -\dfrac{1}{8}$

? Problem

Determine whether these numbers are positive or negative:

$2^2, 2^3, 2^4, 2^5 \ldots$ $(-2)^2, (-2)^3, (-2)^4, (-2)^5 \ldots$

What can you conclude?

A positive number to the power of anything is always positive. A negative number to the power of an odd number is negative, but when it is to the power of an even number it is positive.

Example 2 What number does each of these represent? Are they are positive or negative?

a. $\left(-\dfrac{1}{2}\right)^5$ **b.** $\left(-\dfrac{2}{3}\right)^4$ **c.** $(-1.5)^3$ **d.** $(-1)^{2004}$

Solution

a. $\left(-\dfrac{1}{2}\right)^5 = -\left(\dfrac{1}{2}\right)^5 = -\dfrac{1}{32}$

b. $\left(-\dfrac{2}{3}\right)^4 = \left(\dfrac{2}{3}\right)^4 = \dfrac{2}{3} \times \dfrac{2}{3} \times \dfrac{2}{3} \times \dfrac{2}{3} = \dfrac{16}{81}$ ← Do $-\left(\dfrac{2}{3}\right)^4$ and $\left(-\dfrac{2}{3}\right)^4$ mean the same thing?

c. $(-1.5)^3 = -1.5^3 = -3.375$

d. $(-1)^{2004} = 1^{2004} = 1$

Look for the $\boxed{x^2}$ and $\boxed{x^3}$ keys on your calculator. You can use them to calculate the square and the cube of a number, respectively.

To calculate: 4.32^2

Press the buttons in this order: $\boxed{4}$ $\boxed{\cdot}$ $\boxed{3}$ $\boxed{2}$ $\boxed{x^2}$ $\boxed{=}$

The result is 18.6624

To calculate: 5.11^3

Press the buttons in this order: $\boxed{5}$ $\boxed{\cdot}$ $\boxed{1}$ $\boxed{1}$ $\boxed{x^3}$ $\boxed{=}$

The result is 133.432 831

In general, we use the key $\boxed{x^y}$ to calculate any power of a number.

For example, to calculate: 1.02^{11}

Press the buttons in this order: $\boxed{1}$ $\boxed{\cdot}$ $\boxed{0}$ $\boxed{2}$ $\boxed{x^y}$ $\boxed{1}$ $\boxed{1}$ $\boxed{=}$

The result is 1.243 374 308

Now try using the key $\boxed{x^y}$ to calculate 4.32^2 and 5.11^3.

Practice 5.8

1. Are these calculations correct?

    a. $2^3 = 2 \times 3$ (   )

    b. $2 + 2 + 2 = 2^3$ (   )

    c. $2^3 = 2 \times 2 \times 2$ (   )

    d. $-2^4 = (-2) \times (-2) \times (-2) \times (-2)$ (   )

2. $(-7)^{12}$ is a _____ ('positive' or 'negative') number. $(-12)^9$ is a _____ ('positive' or 'negative') number.

3. Write the numbers represented by these power operations.

    a. $(-1)^{10} =$ _____   **b.** $(-1)^9 =$ _____

    c. $(-3)^3 =$ _____   **d.** $(-5)^2 =$ _____

    e. $(-0.1)^3 =$ _____   **f.** $\left(-\dfrac{1}{2}\right)^4 =$ _____

    g. $-(-1)^{2000} =$ _____   **h.** $-(-0.2)^5 =$ _____

    i. $-\left(-\dfrac{1}{7}\right) =$ _____   **j.** $-\left(-1\dfrac{1}{2}\right)^4 =$ _____

5.9 Mixed operations with rational numbers

You have studied the basic operations: addition, subtraction, multiplication, division and powers as they apply to rational numbers. Which rules do you think mixed operations might follow?

> This is the order of mixed operations for rational numbers: powers is the first step, multiplication or division is the second step, and addition or subtraction is the last step. If there are multiple operations to carry out at the same step, complete them from left to right. **If there are brackets, complete the parts of the equation within the inside (round) brackets first, then complete the parts in the outside (square) brackets and finally the part outside the brackets.**

Example 1   Complete these calculations with mixed operations.

a. $1 - \dfrac{1}{2} + \dfrac{1}{4} - \dfrac{1}{8}$

b. $15 \div (-5 - 3)^2$

c. $3^2 - (-2)^2$

d. $-[-(-2)]^2$

e. $15 - 4 \div 8 + (-3)^2 \times 2$

Solution

a. $1 - \dfrac{1}{2} + \dfrac{1}{4} - \dfrac{1}{8}$

$= \dfrac{1}{2} + \dfrac{1}{4} - \dfrac{1}{8} = \dfrac{3}{4} - \dfrac{1}{8} = \dfrac{5}{8}$

b. $15 \div (-5 - 3)^2$

$= 15 \div (-8)^2 = 15 \div 64 = \dfrac{15}{64}$

c. $3^2 - (-2)^2 = 9 - 4 = 5$

d. $-[-(-2)]^2 = -2^2 = -4$

e. $15 - 4 \div 8 + (-3)^2 \times 2 = 15 - 4 \div 8 + 9 \times 2 = 15 - 0.5 + 18 = 32.5$

Example 2   Solve this calculation: $\dfrac{3}{5} - \left(\dfrac{3}{5} - \dfrac{1}{4} \right)$

Solution 1 $\dfrac{3}{5} - \left(\dfrac{3}{5} - \dfrac{1}{4} \right)$

$= \dfrac{3}{5} - \left(\dfrac{12}{20} - \dfrac{5}{20} \right)$

$= \dfrac{3}{5} - \dfrac{7}{20} = \dfrac{12}{20} - \dfrac{7}{20} = \dfrac{1}{4}$

Solution 2 $\dfrac{3}{5} - \left(\dfrac{3}{5} - \dfrac{1}{4} \right)$

$= \dfrac{3}{5} + (-1) \times \left(\dfrac{3}{5} - \dfrac{1}{4} \right)$

$= \dfrac{3}{5} + (-1) \times \dfrac{3}{5} - (-1) \times \dfrac{1}{4}$

$= \dfrac{3}{5} + \left(-\dfrac{3}{5} \right) - \left(-\dfrac{1}{4} \right)$

$= \dfrac{3}{5} - \dfrac{3}{5} + \dfrac{1}{4} = \dfrac{1}{4}$

Can we remove brackets from a calculation?
If there is a minus sign directly in front of the
brackets, we need to change the sign of each
number within the brackets as we remove them.
For example: $-(a + b) = -a - b$, $-(a - b) = -a + b$.

Practice 5.9 (1)

1. Are these calculations correct? If they are wrong, how would you correct them?

   a. $79 - 3^2 \div 70 = 70 \div 70 = 1$

   b. $6 \div (2 \times 3) = 6 \div 2 \times 3 = 3 \times 3 = 9$

   c. $2 \times 4^2 = (2 \times 4)^2 = 8^2 = 64$

   d. $\dfrac{22}{5} - \left(\dfrac{1}{5} - \dfrac{1}{2}\right) = \dfrac{22}{5} - \dfrac{1}{5} - \dfrac{1}{2} = \dfrac{21}{5} - \dfrac{1}{2} = \dfrac{37}{10}$

2. Solve these calculations with mixed operations.

   a. $(-3) + 2 \times (-4)^2$
      b. $(-32) + (-7) \div \left(-1\dfrac{3}{4}\right)$

   c. $\dfrac{2}{3} - \left(\dfrac{1}{2} - \dfrac{1}{5}\right)$
      d. $(-7) + 5 \times (-6) - (-42) \div (-8)$

   e. $2 \times (-3)^3 - 5 \times (-3) + 25$
      f. $-3^2 - (-2)^2 - (-3)^3 - 2^3$

Example 3   Solve these calculations with mixed operations.

a. $-1^4 - \dfrac{1}{3} \times [2 - (-3)^2]$
      b. $\left(\dfrac{1}{2}\right)^2 + [- (-7) + (-1)^3] \times \dfrac{2}{3}$

c. $\left[\left(\dfrac{1}{8} - \dfrac{1}{12}\right) \times 24\right]^2$
      d. $(-2^3 + 85) \times \left(-3\dfrac{1}{3} + 1 + \dfrac{7}{3}\right)$

Solution

a. $-1^4 - \dfrac{1}{3} \times [2 - (-3)^2]$ ⟵   Note the difference
between -1^4 and $(-1)^4$.

   $= -1 - \dfrac{1}{3} \times (2 - 9) = -1 - \dfrac{1}{3} \times (-7)$

   $= -1 + \dfrac{7}{3} = 1\dfrac{1}{3}$

b. $\left(\dfrac{1}{2}\right)^2 + [- (-7) + (-1)^3] \times \dfrac{2}{3}$

   $= \dfrac{1}{4} + (7 - 1) \times \dfrac{2}{3} = \dfrac{1}{4} + 4 = 4\dfrac{1}{4}$

c. $\left[\left(\dfrac{1}{8} - \dfrac{1}{12}\right) \times 24\right]^2$

$= \left[\left(\dfrac{3}{24} - \dfrac{2}{24}\right) \times 24\right]^2 = \left(\dfrac{1}{24} \times 24\right)^2 = 1^2 = 1$

d. $(-2^3 + 85) \times \left(-3\dfrac{1}{3} + 1 + \dfrac{7}{3}\right)$

$= (-8 + 85) \times \left(-\dfrac{10}{3} + \dfrac{10}{3}\right) = 77 \times 0 = 0$

> We can also use the distributive law to solve the problem:
>
> $\left[\left(\dfrac{1}{8} - \dfrac{1}{12}\right) \times 24\right]^2$
>
> $= \left(\dfrac{1}{8} \times 24 - \dfrac{1}{12} \times 24\right)^2$
>
> $= (3 - 2)^2 = 1^2 = 1$

 Use a calculator to check how it deals with mixed operations on rational numbers. You need to input the numbers and symbols just as they appear in the written calculation. Then press the equals sign to get the result. For example:

> Calculators are designed to follow the order of mixed operations with rational numbers.

Calculate: $(3.2 \times 5.1 - 2.4) \times 3 - 2.1 \div 5$

Press the buttons in this order:

$(\ \boxed{3}\ \boxed{\cdot}\ \boxed{2}\ \boxed{\times}\ \boxed{5}\ \boxed{\cdot}\ \boxed{1}\ \boxed{-}\ \boxed{2}\ \boxed{\cdot}\ \boxed{4}\ )\ \boxed{\times}\ \boxed{3}\ \boxed{-}\ \boxed{2}\ \boxed{\cdot}\ \boxed{1}\ \boxed{\div}\ \boxed{5}\ \boxed{=}$

The result is: 41.34.

Example 4 10 pupils from Year 6 Class 1 take part in a skipping competition at school. These are the total numbers of skips per minute:

124, 115, 112, 125, 120, 118, 130, 108, 114, 127

Find the total number of skips completed by the 10 pupils.

Analysis From the information above, we can see that they all did around 120 skips per minute. So 120 can be used as a standard; we can subtract 120 from each of the results. This means that results greater than 120 will be expressed as positive numbers and results less than 120 will be expressed as negative numbers. We can find the total number of skips completed by the 10 pupils if we work out the sum of the 10 new pieces of data first, then add 120×10 to the result.

Solution 1 Subtract the number of skips for each pupil from 120 to get these numbers: 4, –5, –8, 5, 0, –2, 10, –12, –6, 7

If we then add the ten numbers together, we get:

$4 + (–5) + (– 8) + 5 + 0 + (–2) + 10 + (–12) + (–6) + 7$

$= [(–5) + 5] + [(–8) + (–2) + 10] + [(–6) + 7] + [4 + (–12)]$

$= 1 + (–8) = –7$

If we add –7 and 120×10, we get: ← The commutative and associative laws of addition are being used here.

$(–7) + 120 \times 10 = 1193$

So the total number of skips completed by the 10 pupils was 1193.

> **1.** Why can we use this method to solve the problem?
> **2.** Will the result be different if we change the standard to 119 and run through the operation again?

 Solution 2 Use a calculator:

1	2	4	+	1	1	5	+	1	1	2

+	1	2	5	+	1	2	0	+	1	1	8	+	1	3	0	+

1	0	8	+	1	1	4	+	1	2	7	=

The sum of the 10 results is 1193.

So the total number of skips completed by the 10 pupils was 1193.

Practice 5.9 (2)

1. Calculate.

a. $3 \times [(–2) – 5]^2 – (–4)^3 \div (–8)$

b. $\left[1 – \left(1 – 0.5 \times \dfrac{1}{3}\right)\right] \times [2 – (–3)^2]$

c. $\left(-\dfrac{7}{8} – \dfrac{7}{12}\right) \div \left(-\dfrac{7}{8}\right) + \left(-\dfrac{8}{3}\right)$

d. $\dfrac{5}{18} \times (–36) + \dfrac{15}{16} \times (–8)$

e. $\dfrac{1}{3} \times \dfrac{1}{2} + \left[–13 + \left(-\dfrac{5}{2}\right)\right] \times \dfrac{2}{3}$

f. $\dfrac{12}{5} \times \left(\dfrac{2}{3} – \dfrac{3}{4}\right)$

 2. Use a calculator to find the answers.

a. $\left[\left(\dfrac{2}{3}\right)^2 – \dfrac{3}{4}\right] \times \dfrac{12}{5} + \left(-\dfrac{2}{3}\right)$

b. $0.2^3 + \dfrac{1}{5} \times \dfrac{3}{4} – \dfrac{1}{12}$

5.10 Standard form or scientific notation

The speed of light is about 300 000 000 m/s. It is known that the light emitted from the Sun takes about 500 seconds to travel to the Earth. What is the distance between the Sun and the Earth?

The equation can be written as:
500 × 300 000 000 = 150 000 000 000 m.

Since it is not practical to write this kind of large number, it is usually expressed in the form of a number between 1 and 10, multiplied by 10 to the power of a positive integer. For example:

$300\,000\,000 = 3 \times 100\,000\,000 = 3 \times 10^8$

$150\,000\,000\,000 = 15 \times 10\,000\,000\,000 = 15 \times 10^{10} = 1.5 \times 10^{11}$

This is a useful method for expressing very large or very small numbers.

> This way of writing numbers is called **standard form** or **scientific notation**. The number is written as $a \times 10^n$ ($1 \le |a| < 10$, where n is a positive integer).

> Later you will learn how to write these numbers when n is zero or a negative integer.

Standard form can be used to represent integers, for example, the number 3.2×10^5 is a six-digit integer, 5.107×10^8 is a nine-digit integer. It can also represent decimal numbers, for example, 1.2345×10^2 is 123.45, which is-made up of a three-digit integer and a decimal part

Example 1   Use standard form to express these numbers.

a. 261 500   **b.** −10 200 000   **c.** 5 107 000

Solution

a. $261\,500 = 2.615 \times 10^5$

c. $5\,107\,000 = 5.107 \times 10^6$

b. $-10\,200\,000 = -1.02 \times 10^7$

Example 2 It is known that a person inhales and exhales about 20 000 litres of air a day, so how much air does a person inhale and exhale over the course of a year?

Solution $20\,000 \times 365 = 7\,300\,000 = 7.3 \times 10^6$ (litres)

So a person inhales and exhales about 7.3×10^6 litres of air a year.

Practice 5.10

1. **Use standard form to express these numbers.**

   a. 36 000   **b.** −2 300 000   **c.** 17 020 000

   d. −400 300   **e.** 880 000 000   **f.** −5 635 000

2. **By the end of 2004, the resident population of Shanghai was about 18 000 000. What is the total consumption of Shanghai in a month if each person spends 400 RMB per month? And what is the total consumption in a year? (Use standard form to express the results.)**

3. **An adult's kidneys filter about 2000 litres of blood a day. How much blood does an adult filter per year?**

> **Using standard form on a calculator**
> Try filling the display of your calculator with a number with as many digits as it will take. Then press the $\boxed{=}$ button. Does your calculator change it to a number in standard form?
> Now look to see if your calculator has this button: $\boxed{\text{EXP}}$ If it does, key in 12.3456 $\boxed{\text{EXP}}$ 4. Does it give you 123456? If so, your calculator can work in standard form.

Explore your calculator. If it has a standard form function, use it to check your answers to Question 1 and Question 2.

📝 Unit summary

The content of this unit is intended to increase your knowledge and understanding of numbers. You have learned to recognise positive numbers (positive integers and fractions), negative numbers (negative integers and fractions) and zero. All the positive and negative integers, positive and negative fractions and zero belong to the set of numbers called rational numbers.

The key to learning about positive and negative numbers is understanding opposite numbers and how to use them to analyse problems. You can also understand rational numbers more intuitively and vividly through the concept of the number line.

In the introduction to positive numbers, you understood that the result of addition, multiplication and division of two positive numbers is always positive, but when subtracting two positive numbers, the result is not necessarily positive. Now, after expanding your knowledge to rational numbers, you know two rational numbers are still rational after addition, subtraction, multiplication and division (where the divisor is not zero). In other words, the four operations of addition, subtraction, multiplication and division can be freely applied to rational numbers. Understanding the rules of operations on rational numbers is a basic skill that you will need to master, to be successful in any future study of mathematics. Practice makes perfect and it is important to complete the necessary practice.

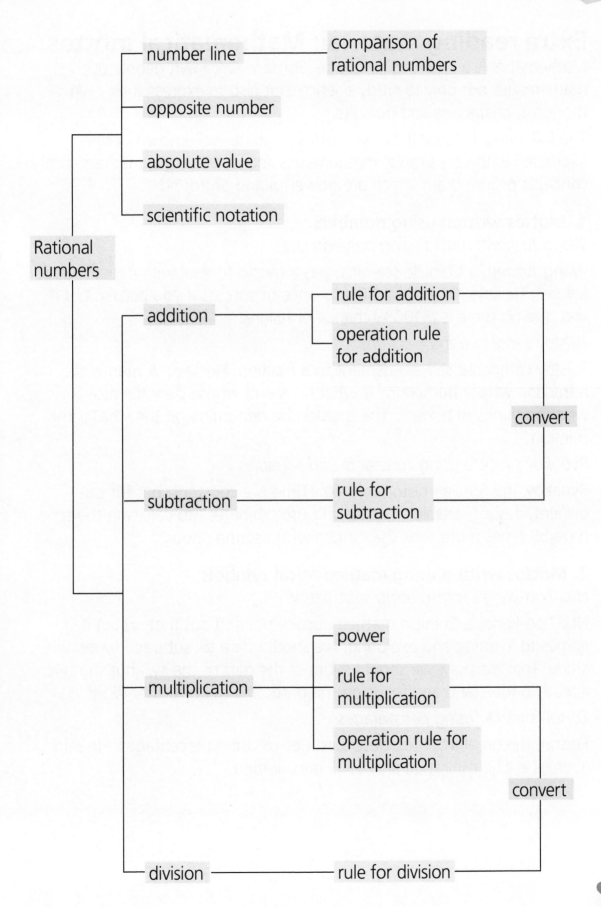

number line —— comparison of rational numbers

opposite number

absolute value

scientific notation

Rational numbers

addition —— rule for addition

operation rule for addition

convert

subtraction —— rule for subtraction

multiplication —— power

rule for multiplication

operation rule for multiplication

convert

division —— rule for division

Extra reading material: Mathematical mottos

Mathematics is a scientific language. Some well-known people use mathematics not only to study science, but also to express their own thoughts, characters and pursuits.

The following list describes the mottos of some well-known people, expressed with very simple 'mathematics' (numbers, signs, mathematical concepts or formulas), which are powerful and profound.

1. Mottos written using numbers

Wang Juzhen's motto using percentages

Wang Juzhen, a Chinese scientist, has a motto to deal with experimental failures. He says: 'There is a 50% chance of success if you persist, but if you give up there is a 100% chance of failure.'

Tolstoy's motto using fractions

Tolstoy compared self-assessment to a fraction. He said: 'A man is like a fraction whose numerator is what he is and whose denominator is what he thinks of himself. The greater the denominator, the smaller the fraction.'

Rybakov's motto using constants and variables

Rybakov, the Russian historian, said: 'Time is a constant, but for the diligent, it is a "variable". Those who use "minutes" to calculate the time have 59 times more time than those who use the "hour".'

2. Mottos written using mathematical symbols

Hua Loo-keng's motto using subtraction

Hua Loo-keng, a Chinese mathematician, pointed out that, when it comes to learning and exploring, we should dare to 'subtract' when we study. That is to say, we should subtract the part of the syllabus that we already understand and focus on the parts that need further work.

Edison's motto using percentages

Edison, the great inventor, described genius using percentages. He said: 'Genius is 1% inspiration and 99% perspiration.'

3. Mottos written using formulas

Einstein's motto using formulas

Einstein, one of the greatest scientists of modern times, used a formula when talking about the secret to success. He said: 'If A is a success in life, then A equals x plus y plus z. Work is x; y is play; and z is keeping your mouth shut.'

Let's enjoy mathematics, learn mathematics, make good use of mathematics and write our own mathematical mottos!

Mathematics game: The 24 points game

Two people are given 20 playing cards each from a pack of cards from which all jacks, queens and kings have been removed. Each round, they should each draw two cards at the same time, spread out the four cards and carry out mixed operations with the numbers on the cards to make a total of 24. (Each card can only be used once and aces count as 1.) The first player to find a way to make 24 is the winner and the loser collects the four cards. If nobody can make 24, each player takes back their own cards. The game ends when one player gets rid of all of their cards.

When Dylan and Emma played, four cards were drawn as follows: ⟶

The equation that Emma came up with was $(3 - 1) \times (7 + 5) = 24$.

Can you think of another way of making 24?

The next four cards were drawn as follows: ⟶

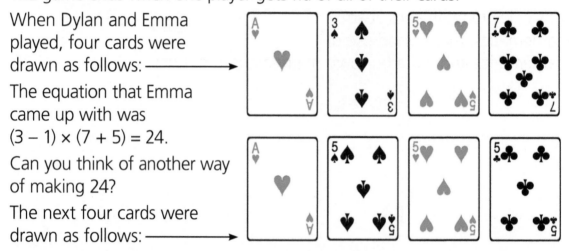

They could not find a way of making 24, so they asked Poppy. Poppy thought for a while and came up with the following equation:

$5 \times (5 - \dfrac{1}{5}) = 24$

After that they had trouble again, with the four cards drawn as follows: ⟶

They discussed their options repeatedly, but still couldn't get a result of 24. They consulted Panda and Panda said: 'You can't get 24 points if you use addition, subtraction, multiplication and division. But if you use powers, you can do it.' Use Panda's suggestion to try making 24.

Panda suggested that you could think of jacks, queens and kings as numbers 11, 12 and 13, respectively. You could also think of the black cards as positive numbers and the red cards as negative ones. This makes it more difficult to apply operations, but you can try mixing and matching different rules.

Unit Six: Linear equations and inequalities

Dylan's family use a variable rate electricity meter, which charges different rates during peak periods and off-peak periods. When the electricity bill comes this month, Dylan's mum gives him some data and tells him to find the unit price of electricity during peak periods and off-peak periods accordingly. How can Dylan calculate this?

The unit price of electricity is 31p lower during off-peak periods than during peak periods.

Section One: Equations and their solutions
6.1 Writing equations

You have already learned some simple equations. Equations play a very important role in mathematics and have a wide application in solving practical problems.

? Problem 1

There are 152 kilograms of bananas and apples in a fruit shop. The mass of apples is three times that of bananas. Find the masses of apples and bananas in the fruit shop.

Analysis 1　We can use what we have learned about fractions and think of the fruit in the fruit shop as a total that is divided into four equal parts.

Each of those parts is $\frac{1}{4}$ of the fruit in the fruit shop, that is $\frac{152}{4} =$ 38 kilograms.

One part is bananas and the other three parts are apples, so the mass of the bananas is 38 kilograms and the mass of the apples is 114 kilograms.

Analysis 2　If the mass of bananas is x kilograms then the mass of apples is $3x$ kilograms. We can write the equivalent equation as:
'The mass of bananas + the mass of apples = total mass'

$3x + x = 152$

$4x = 152$

So we get $x = 38$ and solve the problem.　　← $3x + x = (3 + 1)\,x = 4x$

? Problem 2

A boarding school assigns dormitories at the beginning of term. If each dormitory sleeps 4 pupils there will be 5 dormitories left; if each dormitory sleeps 3 pupils there will be 100 people without beds. How many pupils lodge at the boarding school? Write the equation needed to find the answer.

Analysis　Suppose that y pupils lodge at the school.
Arranging the pupils according to the first method, there are $\left(\frac{y}{4} + 5\right)$ school dormitories; arranging the pupils according to the second method, there are $\frac{y - 100}{3}$ school dormitories. From here we can write the equation:

$$\frac{y}{4} + 5 = \frac{y - 100}{3}$$

? Problem 3

If the sum of a number and its half is $\frac{3}{4}$, what is the number? Write the equation needed to find the answer.

Analysis   If this number is x, then half of it is $\frac{x}{2}$ and the sum of two numbers is $x + \frac{x}{2}$. From here we can write the equation:

$$x + \frac{x}{2} = \frac{3}{4}$$

We use letters such as x and y to represent the numbers you need to find. These letters are called **unknowns**. An equality that contains an unknown is called an **equation**. An unknown contained within an equation is also known as a **variable**.

Deriving an equivalent equation between the unknown and known numbers is known as **writing an equation**.

Example   Write equations for these scenarios.

a. The length of the side of a square is x cm and its perimeter is 36 cm.

b. Poppy got £y pocket money in February. She spent £25.40 and now she has £60 left.

c. Subtracting half of x from $\frac{2}{5}$ equals 56.

Solution

a. The equation is $4x = 36$ **b.** The equation is $y - 25.4 = 60$

c. The equation is $\frac{2}{5} - \frac{x}{2} = 56$

In the equation $y + 2.3 = 0$, $\frac{3}{7} - \frac{x}{2} = 0$, each part that is separated by '+' or '−' (including the signs of '+' and '−', which make a number positive or negative), such as y, 2.3, $\frac{3}{7}$, $-\frac{x}{2}$, is called a **term**. In a term, the number written before the letter(s) denoted is called the **coefficient of the unknown**. For example, the coefficient of y is 1 and the coefficient of $-\frac{x}{2}$ is $-\frac{1}{2}$. In a term, the exponent is called the **power** of this term. For example, the power of both y and $-\frac{x}{2}$ is 1.

A term that does not contain an unknown, such as 2.3 or $\frac{3}{7}$, is known as a **constant term**.

Think!

In the equation $4xy - 5 = 0$, what is the coefficient of $4xy$? What is its power?

Practice 6.1

1. Write the equations.

  a. The sum of $\frac{1}{3}$ of x and 6 is 2.

  b. The opposite number of x minus 5 equals 5.

  c. The cube of y added to x equals 0.

  d. Half of x multiplied by y minus 13 is $\frac{2}{3}$.

2. Choose a letter to represent the unknown in each question, then write a suitable equation.

  a. 2 times a number plus −9 equals 15. Find this number.

  b. The width of a rectangle is one third of its length and its perimeter is 24 cm. Find the length of the rectangle.

  c. Dylan bought 15 exercise books with £10 and received £1 in change. Find the price of one exercise book.

6.2 Solving equations

? Problem

There is a total of 48 pupils in Year 6 Class 2, and there are 8 more girls than boys. How many boys are there in the class?

Analysis If there are x boys, then there are $(x + 8)$ girls, and we can write the equation $x + (x + 8) = 48$.

When we replace x with 20, the values on both sides of the equation are equal. This means that 20 solves the equation $x + (x + 8) = 48$, because one of its solutions is $x = 20$. When we replace x with 19, the values on both sides of the equation are unequal, so 19 is not the solution to the equation $x + (x + 8) = 48$.

> If a value taken by an unknown makes the left and right sides of the equation equal, the value of the unknown is called the **solution to the equation**.

Think!

Is -3 or 1 the solution to the equation $4x^2 - 9 = 2x - 7$?

We can replace x with -3 on the left and right sides of the equation.
The left side $= 4 \times (-3)^2 - 9 = 27$
The right side $= 2 \times (-3) - 7 = -13$
Because the left side $\neq$ the right side
$x = -3$ is not the solution to the equation $4x^2 - 9 = 2x - 7$.

This process is a check.

We can replace x with 1 on the left and right sides of the equation.
The left side $= 4 \times 1^2 - 9 = -5$
The right side $= 2 \times 1 - 7 = -5$
Because the left side $=$ the right side
$x = 1$ is the solution to the equation $4x^2 - 9 = 2x - 7$.

Think!

Is $x = 2$ the solution to the equations

$$3x - 9 = x - 5 \text{ and } \frac{3}{2}x + 18 = \frac{1}{2}x + 20?$$

Practice 6.2

1. Check whether $x = -6$ is the solution to the equation
$5x - 7 = 8x + 11$.

2. Check whether these numbers are solutions to the equation
$\dfrac{2y + 8}{5} = y + \dfrac{5}{2}$.

   a. $y = 0$ **b.** $y = -\dfrac{3}{2}$

3. Check whether $x = 1$ or $x = -2$ are solutions to the equation
$x^2 - 3x + 2 = 0$.

Section Two: Linear equations with one variable

6.3 Solving linear equations with one variable

The perimeter of a rectangular basketball court is 86 metres. Its length is 2 metres less than 2 times its width. What are the length and width of the basketball court in metres?

If the width of the basketball court is x metres, then the length is $(2x - 2)$ metres. From here we get the equation: $2(2x - 2 + x) = 86$.

> If an equation has only one unknown and the power of each unknown is 1, then it is known as a **linear equation with one variable**.

Example 1 Decide whether these equations are linear equations with one variable and, if not, briefly explain why.

a. $5x = 0$

b. $x - 2y = 56$

c. $3 + 5 = 8$

d. $2y - (y + 9) = 15$

Solution

a. Yes.

b. No. This equation contains x and y, two unknowns.

c. No. This equation does not contain unknowns.

d. Yes.

? Problem

How can we solve the equation $x - 9 = 15$?

Because $24 - 9 = 15$, $x = 24$.

I look at the equation as an equality, add 9 to both sides of the equality, then get $x = 24$.

Do you remember the properties of equalities?

Equation property 1: When the same number is added to or subtracted from both sides of an equation, the equation is still true.

Equation property 2: When both sides of a equation are multiplied or divided by the same non-zero number, the equation is still true.

We can find the solution to an equation by using the properties of equalities and operations.

Example 2   Use the properties of equalities to solve this equation.
$4x = 18 - 2x$

Solution   According to the properties of equalities, if $2x$ is added to both sides of the equation, then

$4x + 2x = 18 - 2x + 2x$

$4x + 2x = 18$

$6x = 18$

According to the properties of equalities, if both sides of the equation are divided by 6, then $x = 3$.

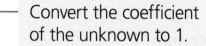 Convert the coefficient of the unknown to 1.

 Are you sure your answer is right?

Replace x with 3 on the left and right sides of the equation and check if their values are equal.

As part of the process above for finding the solution to the equation:

$4x = 18 \boxed{-2x} \longrightarrow 4x \boxed{+2x} = 18$

$-2x$ moves from one side of the equals sign to the other, and changes from negative to positive. This transformation is called **transposition** or **rearranging the terms of an equation**.

The process of finding the solution to an equation is called **solving the equation**.

Practice 6.3 (1)

1. **Decide whether or not these equations are linear equations with one variable.**

   a. $3x = 10$

   b. $5x - \dfrac{4}{7}y = 35$

   c. $x^2 - 14 = 10$

   d. $4z - 3(z - 2) = 1$

2. **Are these processes correct? If not, show where the errors are and correct them.**

   Rearrange $3x - 18 = 9 + 2x$ to give $3x + 2x = 9 - 18$.

   Rearrange $\dfrac{1}{5}x - 12 = x - 5$ to give $5 - 12 = x - \dfrac{1}{5}x$.

3. **Solve the equations.**

   a. $x + 8 = -17$

   b. $3y - 15 = y - 19$

Example 3 Solve this equation: $5x + 1 = 20x - (7x - 3)$

Analysis The equation contains brackets, so remove the brackets first and then find the solution to the equation.

Solution Remove the brackets to give: $5x + 1 = 20x - 7x + 3$

Rearrange the terms to give: $5x - 20x + 7x = 3 - 1$

Simplify to give: $-8x = 2$

Divide both sides of the equation by -8 to get $x = -\dfrac{1}{4}$.

So $x = -\dfrac{1}{4}$ is the solution to the original equation. ← Double-check this.

> The law of transposition: when a plus sign is in front of brackets, all signs within the brackets are unchanged after the brackets are removed. When a minus sign is in front of brackets, all signs within the brackets are changed after the brackets are removed.

Example 4 Solve this equation: $4(x - 2) + 5 = 35 - (x - 2)$

Solution 1 Remove the brackets to give: $4x - 8 + 5 = 35 - x + 2$

Rearrange the terms to give: $4x + x = 35 + 2 + 8 - 5$

Simplify to give: $5x = 40$

Divide both sides of the equation by 5 to get: $x = 8$

So $x = 8$ is the solution to the original equation.

Solution 2 Rearrange the terms
to give: $4(x-2)+(x-2)=35-5$ ← Think of $(x-2)$ as the unknown.
Simplify to give: $5(x-2)=30$
Divide both sides of the equation by 5 to get: $x-2=6$,
$x=8$
So $x=8$ is the solution to the original equation.
Example 5 Solve this equation: $2x-3=3x-(x-2)$
Solution Remove the brackets to give: $2x-3=3x-x+2$
Rearrange the terms and simplify to give: $-3=2$
The equality is false, so the original equation has no solution.

Practice 6.3 (2)

1. Are these calculations correct? If not, show where the errors are and correct them.

a. Remove the brackets in $2(x+4)=9-(x-3)$
to give: $2x+8=9-x-3$
b. Remove the brackets in $15\left(\frac{1}{5}x-1\right)=1-2(x-3)$
to give: $3x-15=1-2x+3$

2. Solve the equations.

a. $7(x-2)=2x-34$

b. $6\left(x+\frac{1}{2}\right)+2=29-3(x-1)$

c. $7(x+3)+4=24-3(x+3)$

Think!

How can we transform the equation $\frac{7x}{20}=\frac{x}{5}+3$ into an equation without fractions?

According to the properties of equalities, we can multiply both sides of the equation by 20 to give:

$20\times\frac{7x}{20}=20\times\frac{x}{5}+20\times3$ ← What's the lowest common multiple of the denominators 20 and 5?
We now have an equation without fractions:
$7x=4x+60$

In the method shown above, we multiplied
both sides of the equation by 20 and removed the fractions. This process is called **simplifying**.

Example 6 Solve this equation: $\dfrac{x}{16} = \dfrac{4x + 5}{8} + 2$

Solution Simplify to give: $x = 2(4x + 5) + 32$ ◄——— Regard the numerator $4x + 5$ as a whole when removing the fractions.

Remove the brackets to give: $x = 8x + 10 + 32$

Rearrange the terms, then simplify to give: $7x = -42$

Divide both sides of the equation by 7 to get: $x = -6$

So $x = -6$ is the solution to the original equation.

The general procedure for solving linear equations with one variable is:
1. Remove the fractions.
2. Remove the brackets.
3. Rearrange the terms.
4. Simplify the form as $ax = b\,(a \neq 0)$.
5. Divide both sides of the equation by the coefficient of the unknown to get the solution in the form $x = \dfrac{b}{a}$.

Practice 6.3 (3)

1. Are these calculations correct? If not, show where the errors are and correct them.

a. Simplify $\dfrac{x}{2} = \dfrac{5x - 17}{4}$ to give: $x = 2(5x - 17)$

b. Simplify $\dfrac{4x - 25}{12} = \dfrac{7x}{6} + \dfrac{1}{2}$
to give: $4x - 25 = 14x + 6$

2. Solve the equations.

a. $\dfrac{x - 9}{4} = \dfrac{x + 5}{3}$

b. $\dfrac{9}{16}x = \dfrac{3}{4}x + 4$

c. $\dfrac{2x - 7}{25} = \dfrac{4x - 13}{75}$

6.4 Applying linear equations with one variable

Think!

Beijing held the Olympics in 2008. In 2004, the Chinese government worked out how to host the Olympics without spending too much money on it. They reduced the budget for the construction of the Beijing National Stadium to 26 hundred million RMB, which was 35% less than the original budget.

What was the original budget for the Beijing National Stadium?

Let's say that the original budget for the Beijing National Stadium was x hundred million RMB. Work on the basis that 'the original budget – the saved fund = the adjusted budget'.

We can write the equation as: $x - 35\%x = 2.6$ ⟵

The solution to the equation is: $x = 4$

So the original budget for the Beijing National Stadium was 4 hundred million RMB.

$$x - 35\%x$$
$$= (1 - 35\%)x$$
$$= \frac{13}{20}x$$

In order to solve word problems, it's often necessary to use appropriate unknowns, write out an equation with the equivalent relationships to the problem and then finally solve it.

> The general procedure for solving word problems with equations:
> **1.** Decide on the unknown(s).
> **2.** Write the equation(s).
> **3.** Solve the equation(s).
> **4.** Check your answer.

Example 1   At the closing ceremony of
the 2004 Athens Olympics, the Chinese
performers took 8 minutes and 49 seconds
to complete a traditional dance, some Chinese
martial arts and one other performance. The
ratio of the times of the three performances was
$10:8:5$. How long did each performance take?

8 minutes and 49 seconds
= 529 seconds

Analysis   By reading the question carefully, we
can work out the word equation:

Time of traditional dance + time of Chinese martial arts +
time of other performance = 529 seconds

Using the ratio of the times of the three performances, we can set the
time for the traditional dance as $10x$ seconds, the time for the Chinese
martial arts as $8x$ seconds and the time for the other performance as
$5x$ seconds.

Solution   Set the time for the traditional dance as $10x$ seconds, the
time for the Chinese martial arts as $8x$ seconds and the time for the other
performance as $5x$ seconds. Using the
information given in the question:

$10x + 8x + 5x = 529$

The solution to the equation is $x = 23$.

So $10x = 230$, $8x = 184$, $5x = 115$.

The traditional dancing took 230
seconds, the Chinese martial arts
took 184 seconds and the other
performance took 115 seconds.

There are relationships between
known and unknown quantities
in many practical problems.
We can use the information
to write an equation, solve
the equation and check the
solution. This method of
solving problems is known as
equational thinking or
equational reasoning.

Practice 6.4 (1)

Solve these word problems using equations.

1. **The Chinese team won 60 gold medals at the 27th and 28th
   Olympics. The ratio of the numbers of gold medals won during
   the 27th and 28th Olympics was 7:8. How many gold medals
   did the Chinese team win at the 27th Olympics?**

2. **Dylan and Emma have 500 books in total. If Emma gave Dylan 15
   books, they would both have the same number of books. How
   many books did Dylan have at the start? How many did Emma
   have?**

? Problem

Emma saved her pocket money and put £300 into a one year fixed-rate bank account in early February. How much will Emma have in the account when the fixed rate expires?

← Look up interest rates of bank savings on the internet.

Facts about savings deposits:
Interest = original deposit × interest rate × period of time
Pre-tax amount = original deposit + interest
After-tax amount = original deposit + interest (after tax)
After-tax interest = interest − interest tax paid

Example 2   Dylan's mother put £5000 in the bank. The government's tax on savings interest is: interest tax = savings interest × 20%. The bank collects it when the depositor withdraws money. If Dylan's mother saves this money for one year, she can get £5090 back. So what is the annual rate of interest?

Solution   Set the annual rate as x. From the information in the problem: $5000 + 5000 \times x \times 1 \times (1 - 20\%) = 5090$

The solution to the equation is: $x = 0.0225$

So $x = 2.25\%$

So the annual rate of interest is 2.25%.

Example 3   A home electricals shop is selling a refrigerator for £486, which includes a discount of 10% off its usual price. The shop will still make a profit because they set the usual price by increasing the wholesale price by 20%. What was the wholesale price of the refrigerator? If the shop sells at the new price, how much do they earn from selling each refrigerator?

Solution   Set the refrigerator's wholesale price as x pounds, so the original price is £$(1 + 20\%)x$. From the information in the problem:

$(1 + 20\%)x \times 90\% = 486$

The solution to the equation is: $x = 450$ $486 - 450 = 36$

So the refrigerator's wholesale price was £450. If the shop sells at the new price, they can earn £36 from each refrigerator.

Example 4 Emma and Poppy are practising a running and walking race on a 400 metre circular race track. Emma runs 320 metres per minute. Poppy walks 120 metres per minute. If they start from the same point at the same time and go in the same direction, how long will it take for them to meet again?

Analysis Emma and Poppy started from the same point at the same time and went in the same direction, so their next meeting will be when Emma laps Poppy. The word equation is:

the distance Emma ran − the distance Poppy walked = 400

We know that 'speed × time = distance', so we can find the third quantity if we already have two of the quantities.

Solution Let's say that Poppy and Emma meet after x minutes.

$320x - 120x = 400$

The solution to the equation is: $x = 2$

So they meet again after 2 minutes.

Practice 6.4 (2)

1. The annual interest rate on savings for a bank is 2.25%. When Poppy's father withdrew his money (the original deposit plus the interest) from the bank one year after making a deposit, £27 interest tax was deducted. How much was Poppy's father's original deposit?

2. A fabric shop sets the selling price of a certain type of fabric by increasing the cost price by 40%. In a sale the shop sells the cloth at 20% off. The shop can still earn £15 for each piece of fabric. What was the cost price?

3. Dylan and Poppy are practising running on a circular race track of circumference 400 metres. Poppy runs 220 metres per minute. Dylan runs 280 metres per minute. If they start from the same point at the same time but in opposite directions, how long will it take for them to meet again?

4. A school had a model aircraft competition. The first model aircraft flew 480 metres less than the second one. The first model aircraft flew at a speed of 1 metre per second faster than the second. The two model aircraft flew in the sky for 12 minutes and 16 minutes respectively. How far did they fly?

Section Three: Linear inequalities with one variable

6.5 Inequalities and their properties

Think!

Look at the traffic signs in the picture. What do the signs with numbers on them indicate?

The mass of the vehicle must not exceed 5 tonnes; the height of the vehicle must not exceed 4 metres; the speed of the vehicle must not exceed 40 miles per hour.

We can use mathematical notation to express this information:
$p \leqslant 5t$; $h \leqslant 4$ m; $v \leqslant 40$ mph
where 'p' is mass, 'h' is height and 'v' is speed.

What is the meaning of the symbol $\leqslant$?

We call this type of formula an **inequality**. We can recognise an inequality because it will make use of one or more of the inequality symbols: $>$, $<$, $\leqslant$ or $\geqslant$.

When comparing two rational numbers, we use the inequality signs $>$ or $<$. For example, $15 > 7$ or $8 < 29$.

Example 1 Use inequalities to express these statements.

a. The sum of a and b is less than 0.

b. Half of x minus 3 is more than or equal to -5.

Solution

a. $a + b < 0$

b. $\dfrac{x}{2} - 3 \geqslant -5$

Observation

Add three weights to both sides of the balance; take away one weight from both sides of the balance; observe the balance indicator.

Can you write the corresponding inequalities?

$5 > 4, 5 + 3 > 4 + 3, 5 - 1 > 4 - 1$

The first property of inequalities: If we add or subtract the same number (or other term) to both sides of an inequality, the inequality will still be true.

If $a > b$, then $a + m > b + m$

If $a > b$, then $a - m > b - m$

Practice 6.5 (1)

1. Use inequalities to express these statements.

   a. The sum of a and 5 is more than -3.

   b. 4 times a number is less than or equal to 12.

   c. 3 times a number minus 2 is a non-negative number.

   d. Half of b is less than the product of a and b.

2. Fill in the correct inequality signs.

   a. If $a < 0$, $b > 0$, then ab ___ 0

   c. If $a > b$, then $a + 5$ ___ $b + 5$

   e. If $4x \leqslant 1$, then $4x + 2$ ___ 3

   b. If $a < 0$, b ___ 0, then $ab > 0$

   d. If $\frac{x}{2} < \frac{y}{2}$, then $\frac{x}{2} - 3$ ___ $\frac{y}{2} - 3$

Think!

Mrs Richards and Miss Khan both live 6 km away from school. They leave work together at the same time to cycle home. Their respective cycling speeds are 0.2 km per minute and 0.15 km per minute. After 10 minutes, who is further away from the school? Who is further away from home?

> $0.2 > 0.15$. Which is greater, 0.2×10 or 0.15×10?
>
> Which is greater, $6 - 0.2 \times 10$ or $6 - 0.15 \times 10$?

The second property of inequalities: If we multiply or divide both sides of an inequality by the same positive number, the inequality will still be true.

If $a > b$, $m > 0$, then $am > bm$ $\left(\text{or } \dfrac{a}{m} > \dfrac{b}{m}\right)$

If $a < b$, $m > 0$, then $am < bm$ $\left(\text{or } \dfrac{a}{m} < \dfrac{b}{m}\right)$

The third property of inequalities: If we multiply or divide both sides of an inequality by the same negative number, the inequality sign will be reversed.

If $a > b$, $m < 0$, then $am < bm$ $\left(\text{or } \dfrac{a}{m} < \dfrac{b}{m}\right)$

If $a < b$, $m < 0$, then $am > bm$ $\left(\text{or } \dfrac{a}{m} > \dfrac{b}{m}\right)$

What will happen if we multiply both sides of the inequality by zero?

Example 2 If $a < b$, write in the inequality signs and decide which of the properties of inequalities applies.

a. $3a$ ____ $3b$ (The _____ property of inequalities)

b. $a - \dfrac{2}{5}$ ____ $b - \dfrac{2}{5}$ (The _____ property of inequalities)

c. $-2a$ ____ $-2b$ (The _____ property of inequalities)

Solution

a. $3a < 3b$ (The second property of equalities)

b. $a - \dfrac{2}{5} < b - \dfrac{2}{5}$ (The first property of equalities)

c. $-2a > -2b$ (The third property of equalities)

Think!

If $a > b$, $m \neq 0$, is it always the case that $am > bm$? Can you illustrate why?

Practice 6.5 (2)

1. If $a < b$, write in the inequality signs and decide which of the properties of inequalities applies.

a. $-5a$ ____ $-5b$ (The _____ property of inequalities)

b. $a + \dfrac{3}{8}$ ____ $b + \dfrac{3}{8}$ (The _____ property of inequalities)

c. $9a$ ____ $9b$ (The _____ property of inequalities)

d. $-a$ ____ $-b$ (The _____ property of inequalities)

2. Explain how to transform these inequalities.

a. From $2x^2 + 13 > 20$ to $2x^2 > 7$

b. From $-5y > 45$ to $y < -9$

c. From $-5 > 2a$ to $a < -\dfrac{5}{2}$

6.6 Solving linear inequalities with one variable

Think!

What are the height restrictions for a vehicle on a road with this traffic sign? What are all of the heights that vehicles driving on this road could be?

1.6 m, 2.7 m, 3 m, $3\frac{1}{3}$ m…

The solution to the inequality is the set of all the values of the unknowns that could make the inequality true.

For example, solutions to $x < 4$ include 1, 1.5, 3.4, 0.3, −5, −10.4, -10^8 … We can replace x with any number less than 4 and the inequality is true. So the number of solutions to the inequality $x < 4$ is infinite.

We call all of the possible solutions to one inequality the **solution set of the inequality**.

In general, linear equations with one variable only have one solution, while the number of solutions to linear inequalities with one variable is infinite.

We can use a number line to show the solution set of the inequality directly, for example:

The solution set for $x < 4$ is shown with an open circle on the number line*.

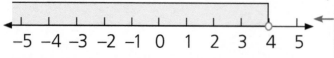

One of these two inequality signs (> or <) before the number 4 means that the solution set does not include the number 4.

The solution set for $x \geqslant -5$ is shown with a filled circle on the number line.

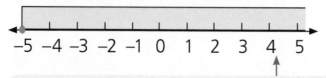

One of these two inequality signs ($\geqslant$ or $\leqslant$) before the number −5 means that the solution set does include the number −5.

* The solution set of $x < 4$ contains infinitely many rational numbers and also infinitely many irrational numbers such as π. You will learn more about this later.

? Problem

A reservoir is being built. It is a cuboid with a length of 5 metres and a width of 4 metres. If the reservoir must contain at least 50 cubic metres of water, what is its shallowest possible depth?

If we set the depth of the reservoir as x metres, we get this inequality:

$4 \times 5 \times x \geqslant 50$

By using the properties of inequalities, we get the solution set $x \geqslant 2.5$.

So the depth of the reservoir must be at least 2.5 m.

> We call the process of finding the solution set of an inequality **solving the inequality**.

Example 1   Find the solution set for each inequality and show it on a number line.

a. $x - 2 < 0$

b. $3x \geqslant -15$

> We use an open circle, o, if the sign is < or >, and a solid or filled circle, •, if the sign is ⩽ or ⩾.

Solution

a. Add 2 to both sides of the inequality:

$x - 2 + 2 < 0 + 2$

$x < 2$

Show this on the number line as:

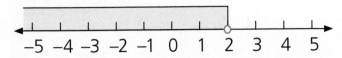

$$-5 \quad -4 \quad -3 \quad -2 \quad -1 \quad 0 \quad 1 \quad 2 \quad 3 \quad 4 \quad 5$$

b. Divide both sides of the inequality by 3:

$3x \div 3 \geqslant (-15) \div 3$

$x \geqslant -5$

Show this on the number line as:

$$-5 \quad -4 \quad -3 \quad -2 \quad -1 \quad 0 \quad 1 \quad 2 \quad 3 \quad 4 \quad 5$$

Example 2 Write one inequality that meets each of the conditions of the solution set shown on the number line.

a.

$$-5 \;-4 \;-3 \;-2 \;-1 \;\;0 \;\;1 \;\;2 \;\;3 \;\;4 \;\;5$$

b.

$$-5 \;-4 \;-3 \;-2 \;-1 \;\;0 \;\;1 \;\;2 \;\;3 \;\;4 \;\;5$$

Solution

a. $x > -3$

b. $x \leqslant 4$

a. Could it be $-x < 3$ or $2x > -6$?

b. Could it be $2x \leqslant 8$ or $x - 2 \leqslant 2$?

Practice 6.6 (1)

1. Find the solution set for each inequality and show it on a number line.

   a. $x + 1 < 3$

   b. $4x \geqslant -28$

   c. $3y - 11 > -2$

   d. $z - 2\dfrac{2}{5} \leqslant 7\dfrac{3}{5}$

2. Find which of these numbers makes each inequality true as x: **−3, −1, 0, 4 or 8.**

   a. $5x + 12 < 0$

   b. $x - 3 \geqslant 4$

   c. $-4x \leqslant -16$

   d. $\dfrac{3}{4}x > \dfrac{1}{4}x - 2$

3. Write an inequality that meets the requirements for each of the solution sets shown on the number lines.

   a.

$$-5 \;-4 \;-3 \;-2 \;-1 \;\;0 \;\;1 \;\;2 \;\;3 \;\;4 \;\;5$$

   b.

$$-5 \;-4 \;-3 \;-2 \;-1 \;\;0 \;\;1 \;\;2 \;\;3 \;\;4 \;\;5$$

Think!

Dylan, Emma and Poppy are representing their class in their school's general knowledge competition. Dylan got 75 points and Emma got 82 points. What score does Poppy need to get if their team needs at least 240 points to win?

Let's say that Poppy gets x points, from which we can write this inequality:

$75 + 82 + x \geqslant 240$

What are the properties of this kind of inequality?

When an inequality contains only one variable, and the power of each variable is 1, we call it a **linear inequality with one variable**.

To find the solution set of $75 + 82 + x \geqslant 240$ is to solve a linear inequality with one variable. Can you solve it?

$75 + 82 + x \geqslant 240$

$157 + x \geqslant 240$

Subtract 157 from both sides of the inequality to give

Do you remember the steps for solving linear equations with one variable?

$x \geqslant 83$

So Poppy must get 83 points or more if their team's score is to be more than or equal to 240 points.

The steps for solving a linear inequality with one variable are similar to the steps for solving a linear equation with one variable:
1. Remove any fractions.
2. Remove the brackets.
3. Rearrange the terms.
4. Rearrange the form to $ax > b$ (or $ax < b$) ($a \neq 0$).
5. Divide both sides of the inequality by the coefficient of the unknown.

Example 3   Solve the inequality $3x + 12 > 40 - x$ and show it on a number line.

Solution   Rearrange the terms to get $3x + x > 40 - 12$.

$4x > 28$

Divide both sides of the inequality by the coefficient of x: $x > 7$.

Show this on a number line:

When we divide both sides of the inequality by the coefficient 4, the direction of the inequality sign does not change.

Example 4   Solve the inequality $4x - 10 < 15x - (8x - 2)$ and show its solution set on a number line.

Solution   Remove the brackets to give $4x - 10 < 15x - 8x + 2$.

Rearrange the terms to give $4x - 15x + 8x < 2 + 10$.

Simplify to give $-3x < 12$.

Divide both sides by the coefficient -3 to get $x > -4$.

When we divide both sides of the inequality by the coefficient -3, we need to change the inequality sign.

The solution set of the inequality shown on a number line is:

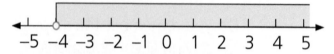

Practice 6.6 (2)

1. Decide whether each of these equalities is a linear inequality with one variable. If it is not, explain your reason briefly.

   a. $16x < 0$

   b. $3x - y < 56$

   c. $2y - (y - 9) < -1$

   d. $x^2 \geqslant 35$

2. Solve each inequality and show its solution set on a number line.

   a. $7x < 6x - 3$

   b. $5x - 12 < 8x - 33$

   c. $\dfrac{5}{4}x + 4 \leqslant \dfrac{9}{4}x - 1$

   d. $3(6x + 7) \geqslant 8 - 2(5x - 9)$

Example 5 Solve the inequality $\dfrac{2x-5}{16} \geqslant \dfrac{4x+5}{2}$ and show its solution set on a number line.

Solution Remove the fractions to give $2x - 5 \geqslant 8 \times (4x + 5)$.

Remove the brackets to give $2x - 5 \geqslant 32x + 40$.

Rearrange the terms and simplify to give $-30x \geqslant 45$.

Divide both sides by the coefficient -30 to get $x \leqslant -\dfrac{3}{2}$.

← Do you remember how to solve the equation $\dfrac{2x-5}{16} = \dfrac{4x+5}{2}$?

The solution set of the inequality shown on a number line is:

Example 6 284 pupils and teachers in Year 6 are going on a school trip by bus. If every bus takes 48 people, what is the minimum number of buses required?

Solution Set up the minimum number of buses as x and you can draw up the inequality:

$48x \geqslant 284$

From there you can solve x: $x \geqslant \dfrac{71}{12}$

The question requires the minimum positive integer for which the inequality holds, so $x = 6$. So the minimum number of buses required is 6.

← Pay attention to the real-life applications of the problem.

Practice 6.6 (3)

1. Solve each inequality and show its solution set on a number line.

a. $\dfrac{7x-13}{6} > \dfrac{3x-8}{3}$

b. $\dfrac{5}{7}x + \dfrac{2}{3} < \dfrac{x+12}{21}$

c. $3 - \dfrac{x-2}{2} \leqslant \dfrac{1}{6}x$

2. Find the negative integer solutions to the inequality $4 - 7x < 41 + 3x$.

6.7 Systems of linear inequalities with one variable

 ## Think!

A shop can buy a toaster for a wholesale (cost) price of £30. If they sell it at 12% off the normal selling price, they will still make at least 10% profit. If they sell it at 10% off the normal selling price, they make less than 20% profit. What is the normal selling price?

> Think about it – how can we use inequalities to express this?

Set the normal selling price as £x and use the information in the question to write these two inequalities.

Selling at 12% off: $x \times \dfrac{88}{100} \geqslant 30(1 + \dfrac{10}{100})$

So $\dfrac{88x}{100} \geqslant 30 \times \dfrac{110}{100}$ or $88x \geqslant 3300$

Selling at 10% off: $x \times \dfrac{90}{100} < 30(1 + \dfrac{20}{100})$

So $\dfrac{90x}{100} < 30 \times \dfrac{120}{100}$ or $9x < 360$

> A set of linear inequalities with the same unknown is called a **system of linear inequalities with one variable**. The set of solutions that satisfy all of the inequalities is called the **solution set for the system of inequalities**. Working out the solution set for the system of inequalities is known as **solving the system of inequalities**.

How can we find the solution set for this system of inequalities?

| Find the solution sets for each inequality in the system. | Show every solution set for the inequalities on the same number line. | Find which part of the solution sets is shared. |

$\begin{cases} 88x \geqslant 3300 \\ 9x < 360 \end{cases}$

The solution set for the inequality $88x \geqslant 3300$ is $x \geqslant 37.5$ and the solution set for the inequality $9x < 360$ is $x < 40$. The two solution sets for the inequalities are shown on the same number line as:

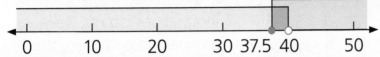

The shared (overlapping) part of the two solution sets on the number line is the solution set for the system of inequalities. We write this set of values for x as: $37.5 \leqslant x < 40$

So the original selling price for the toaster was between £37.50 and £40.

Example 1   Find the solution sets for these systems of inequalities and show them on number lines.

a. $\begin{cases} x > 4 \\ x > 12 \end{cases}$
b. $\begin{cases} x < 4 \\ x < -3 \end{cases}$
c. $\begin{cases} x < 4.5 \\ x > -3 \end{cases}$
d. $\begin{cases} x > 4 \\ x < -3\frac{1}{2} \end{cases}$

Solution

a. Show the solution sets for $x > 4$ and $x > 12$ on a number line.

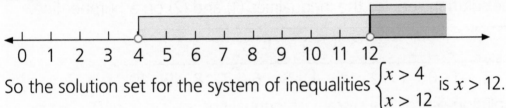

So the solution set for the system of inequalities $\begin{cases} x > 4 \\ x > 12 \end{cases}$ is $x > 12$.

b. Show the solution sets for $x < 4$ and $x < -3$ on a number line.

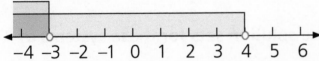

So the solution set for the system of inequalities $\begin{cases} x < 4 \\ x < -3 \end{cases}$ is $x < -3$.

c. Show the solution sets for $x < 4.5$ and $x > -3$ on a number line.

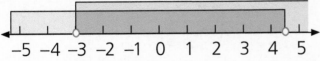

So the solution set for the system of inequalities $\begin{cases} x < 4.5 \\ x > -3 \end{cases}$ is $-3 < x < 4.5$.

d. Show the solution sets for $x > 4$ and $x < -3\frac{1}{2}$ on a number line.

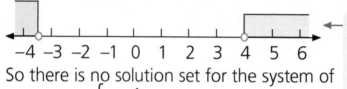

So there is no solution set for the system of inequalities $\begin{cases} x > 4 \\ x < -3\frac{1}{2} \end{cases}$

← If the solution sets for the inequalities do not have any part in common, the system of inequalities has no solution set.

Example 2 Find a solution set for this system of inequalities:

$$\begin{cases} 4x > 2x - 6 & (1) \\ 10 + 3x > 7x - 30 & (2) \end{cases}$$

Solution From (1) we get $2x > -6$.

So $x > -3$

From (2) we get $-4x > -40$

So $x < 10$

Show the solution sets for the inequalities (1) and (2) on a number line.

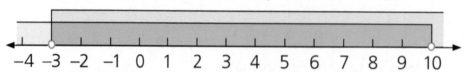

So the solution set for the system of inequalities is $-3 < x < 10$.

✎ Practice 6.7 (1)

1. Use a number line to find the solution sets for these systems of inequalities.

a. $\begin{cases} x > 0 \\ x > 2 \end{cases}$

b. $\begin{cases} x < 1\frac{1}{2} \\ x < -5 \end{cases}$

c. $\begin{cases} x \leqslant 2\frac{1}{3} \\ x > -0.5 \end{cases}$

d. $\begin{cases} x \geqslant -7 \\ x \leqslant 2\frac{2}{3} \end{cases}$

2. Solve these systems of inequalities.

a. $\begin{cases} 3x - 5 > 2x - 1 \\ 5x - 6 > 2x \end{cases}$

b. $\begin{cases} 5 - 2x < 2x - 1 \\ x + 3 > 2x \end{cases}$

Example 3   Solve this system of inequalities: $\begin{cases} \dfrac{5-2x}{4} > \dfrac{3-2x}{6} & (1) \\ 5x \leqslant x - 14 & (2) \end{cases}$

Solution   From (1) we get $15 - 6x > 6 - 4x$

So $x < \dfrac{9}{2}$

From (2) we get $4x \leqslant -14$

So $x \leqslant -\dfrac{7}{2}$

Show the solution sets for the inequalities (1) and (2) on a number line:

← When each side of the inequality (1) is multiplied by 12, which is the lowest common multiple of 4 and 6, you do not need to change the inequality sign.

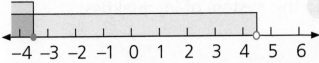

So the solution set for the system of inequalities is $x \leqslant -\dfrac{7}{2}$.

Example 4   Find the integer solutions to this system of inequalities:
$\begin{cases} 5x - 10 > 2x - 4 \\ 3(x-2) + 4 \leqslant 25 - (x+6) \end{cases}$

Solution   The system of inequalities $\begin{cases} 5x - 10 > 2x - 4 & (1) \\ 3(x-2) + 4 \leqslant 25 - (x+6) & (2) \end{cases}$

From (1) we get $x > 2$

From (2) we get $x \leqslant \dfrac{21}{4}$

Show the solution sets for the inequalities (1) and (2) on a number line:

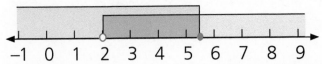

So the solution set for the system of inequalities is $2 < x \leqslant \dfrac{21}{4}$ and its integer solutions are 3, 4 and 5.

Summary

The general procedure for solving a system of linear inequality with one variable is:
1. Find the solution sets of each inequality in the system of inequalities.
2. Show all the solution sets for the inequalities on a number line.
3. Identify the shared parts of the different solution sets to find the solution set for the system of inequalities.

✏ Practice 6.7 (2)

1. Solve these systems of inequalities.

a. $\begin{cases} 16x > 24x - 32 \\ 9x > 7x - 6 \end{cases}$

b. $\begin{cases} 2(x - 4) \leqslant x - 6 \\ 4 + x > 5x - 24 \end{cases}$

c. $\begin{cases} \dfrac{x - 7}{15} < \dfrac{x - 2}{5} \\ \dfrac{1}{2}x - 1 \leqslant 3 - \dfrac{3}{2}x \end{cases}$

2. Find the integer solutions to this system of inequalities.

$\begin{cases} 7(x - 1) < 4x + 3 \\ 6(\dfrac{2}{3}x + 1) \geqslant 2x - 5 \end{cases}$

Section Four: Linear equations with two or more variables

6.8 Linear equations with two variables

❓ Problem

Poppy bought a bouquet of flowers for her mother's birthday. The bouquet was made up of red and pink carnations, and cost £10. Given that red carnations cost 70p each and pink carnations cost 50p each, how many red carnations and how many pink carnations could there be in the bouquet of flowers?

Set the number of red carnations as x and the number of pink carnations as y, which leads to the equation:

$0.7x + 0.5y = 10$ (where x and y are positive integers)

So $7x + 5y = 100$
(where x and y are positive integers)

> How is this equation the same as or different from a linear equation with one variable?

> A linear equation with two unknown numbers is called a **linear equation with two variables**.

In the equation $7x + 5y = 100$, x and y are positive integers. Based on the price of red carnations, we can write the inequality $0 < 7x < 100$ or $0 < x < \dfrac{100}{7}$, so x may be any positive integer from 1 to 14. Then we can draw a table of values.

x	1	2	...	5	6	...	10	11	...	14
y	$\dfrac{93}{5}$	$\dfrac{86}{5}$	...	13	$\dfrac{58}{5}$	...	6	$\dfrac{23}{5}$	...	$\dfrac{2}{5}$

> Change $7x + 5y = 100$ to $y = \dfrac{100 - 7x}{5}$, so each x value corresponds to a y value.

The pairs of values of x and y, which must be whole numbers to answer the question, are 5 and 13, and 10 and 6, which you can write as:

$$\begin{cases} x = 5 \\ y = 13 \end{cases} \qquad \begin{cases} x = 10 \\ y = 6 \end{cases}$$

So Poppy bought 5 red carnations and 13 pink carnations, or 10 red carnations and 6 pink carnations.

The values of the two unknown numbers that make both sides of the linear equation with two variables equal are called the **solution to the linear equation with two variables**.

There are only two positive integer solutions to the equation $7x + 5y = 100$, but if you don't take account of the real-life context of the question, does it have any other solutions? How many?

The equation $7x + 5y = 100$ has an infinite number of solutions.

The number of solutions to a linear equation with two variables is infinite. The full set of solutions to the linear equation with two variables is called the **solution set for the linear equation with two variables**.

Example 1 Rearrange $36x - 4y = 56$ to give an equation for y in terms of x. Solve for y when $x = 2$ or -5.

Solution Rearrange the terms to give $4y = 36x - 56$, which simplifies to give: $y = 9x - 14$

Set $x = 2$ and $x = -5$ in the equation $y = 9x - 14$ to give:

$y = 9 \times 2 - 14 = 4$

$y = 9 \times (-5) - 14 = -59$

So when $x = 2$ and -5, y equals 4 and when $x = -5$, $y = -59$.

Example 2 Find the positive integer solutions to this linear equation with two variables: $x + 4y = 16$

Analysis There are infinitely many solutions to the equation $x + 4y = 16$, but the number of positive integer solutions is limited. We should think about the positive integers when $0 < y < 4$ (or $0 < x < 16$).

Solution Rearrange the terms to give: $x = 16 - 4y$ (1)

Put $y = 1$, $y = 2$ and $y = 3$, in turn, in (1) to find the values of x.

$x = 16 - 4 \times 1 = 12 \qquad x = 16 - 4 \times 2 = 8 \qquad x = 16 - 4 \times 3 = 4$

So the positive integer solutions to the linear equation with two variables $x = 16 - 4y$ are:

$$\begin{cases} x = 12 \\ y = 1 \end{cases} \qquad \begin{cases} x = 8 \\ y = 2 \end{cases} \qquad \begin{cases} x = 4 \\ y = 3 \end{cases}$$

Practice 6.8

1. Rearrange the terms in $5x + y = 11$ to give an equation for y in terms of x. Solve for y when $x = -1$ and $x = \dfrac{3}{10}$.

2. Rearrange the terms in $3x - 2y = 25$ to give an equation for x in terms of y. Solve for x when $y = -4$ and $y = 7$.

3. Find the positive integer solutions to the linear equation with two variables $5x + y = 15$.

4. Find the negative integer solutions to the linear equation with two variables $2x + y = -7$.

6.9 Solving systems of linear equations with two variables

? Problem

An ancient Chinese mathematics book called *Sunzi's Mathematical Classic* recorded an interesting problem about chickens and rabbits, as follows: A number of chickens and how many rabbits are in the same enclosure. There are 35 heads and 94 feet, so how many chickens and rabbits are there in the enclosure?

If we set the number of chickens as x and the number of rabbits as y, we can use the question to write the equations $x + y = 35$ and $2x + 4y = 94$. Write them together as:

$$\begin{cases} x + y = 35 \\ 2x + 4y = 94 \end{cases}$$

> A set of several related equations is called a **system of equations**. If there are two unknown numbers in the system of equations, and the power of each variable is 1, the system is known as a **system of linear equations with two variables**.

List the solutions to the equation $x + y = 35$, as follows:

x	...	22	23	24	25	...
y	...	13	12	11	10	...

List the solutions to the equation $2x + 4y = 94$, as follows:

x	...	22	23	24	25	...
y	...	12.5	12	11.5	11	...

From the table we can see that $x = 23$ and $y = 12$ are solutions to both the equation $x + y = 35$ and the equation $2x + 4y = 94$, so the solution to the system of linear equations with two variables is:

$$\begin{cases} x + y = 35 \\ 2x + 4y = 94 \end{cases}$$
$$\begin{cases} x = 23 \\ y = 12 \end{cases}$$

In a system of linear equations with two variables, the solution that works for every equation in the system is the **solution to the system of linear equations with two variables**.

Think!

Dylan went to the sports shop to buy shuttlecocks and table tennis balls. He needs to buy twice as many shuttlecocks as table tennis balls. The shop sells each shuttlecock for £1 and each table tennis ball for 20p. Dylan spent £4.40 in all. How many shuttlecocks and how many table tennis balls has Dylan bought?

Set the number of shuttlecocks as x and the number of table tennis balls as y, and use the question to write the system of equations:

$$\begin{cases} x = 2y & (1) \\ x + 0.2y = 4.4 & (2) \end{cases}$$

Should we find the solutions to each equation in the system of equations and then spot the solution that works for all of them?

We could replace the x in equation (2) with the $2y$ in equation (1) to give a linear equation with one variable about y. We can solve that!

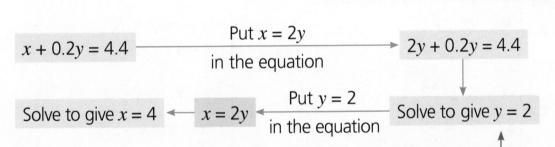

| $x + 0.2y = 4.4$ | Put $x = 2y$ in the equation | $2y + 0.2y = 4.4$ |

| Solve to give $x = 4$ | $x = 2y$ | Put $y = 2$ in the equation | Solve to give $y = 2$ |

The solution to the equation is $\begin{cases} x = 4 \\ y = 2 \end{cases}$

So Dylan bought 4 shuttlecocks and 2 table tennis balls with £4.40.

Working out the solution to a system of equations is known as **solving the system of equations**.

Example 1 Solve this system of equations: $\begin{cases} 3x - y = 5 & (1) \\ 4x + 2y = 11 & (2) \end{cases}$

Solution From (1) we get: $y = 3x - 5$ (3)

Put the value of y in (3) into (2) to give

$4x + 2(3x - 5) = 11$

Solve to give: $x = \dfrac{21}{10}$

Put $x = \dfrac{21}{10}$ into (3) to give: $y = 3 \times \dfrac{21}{10} - 5$

Solve to give: $y = \dfrac{13}{10}$

So the solution to the system of equations is: $\begin{cases} x = \dfrac{21}{10} \\ y = \dfrac{13}{10} \end{cases}$

> Putting a value for one of the unknowns into an equation is called substitution.

> Through substitution we can eliminate an unknown number and turn the system of equations into a linear equation with one variable. This is known as **elimination by substitution** and is also referred to as the **substitution elimination method**.

Practice 6.9 (1)

1. Which of these systems of equations are systems of linear equations with two variables?

a. $\begin{cases} 5x + 6y = 21 \\ xy = -2 \end{cases}$

b. $\begin{cases} 14x = -9y + 76 \\ y = -8 \end{cases}$

c. $\begin{cases} x^2 - 4y = \dfrac{44}{3} \\ 3y - 9x = -5 \end{cases}$

d. $\begin{cases} \dfrac{3}{4}x - 5y = 1.2 \\ 22x - 11y = -5.5 \end{cases}$

2. Solve these systems of equations.

a. $\begin{cases} 7x - 3y = 54 \\ y = -20 \end{cases}$

b. $\begin{cases} 8x - 3y = 11 \\ x - y = -8 \end{cases}$

c. $\begin{cases} \dfrac{1}{4}x - 3y = 8 \\ y - 2x = 5 \end{cases}$

d. $\begin{cases} \dfrac{7}{2}x - y = \dfrac{3}{2} \\ 3x + 2y = -8 \end{cases}$

Think!

How can we solve this system of equations? $\begin{cases} x - 2y = 6 \\ 3x + 2y = 10 \end{cases}$

Express x as $2y + 6$ from the first equation, and then substitute this into the second equation to give a linear equation with one variable, y.

What do you notice about the coefficients of the unknowns and their signs in this system of equations?

Add the two equations together in the system of equations to eliminate y and give a linear equation with one variable, x.

When the coefficients of one of the variables in a system of equations are the same, we can add or subtract the equations to eliminate that unknown number and change the system of equations into a linear equation with one variable. This method of solution is known as **elimination by adding or subtracting**.

Example 2   Solve this system of equations: $\begin{cases} 2x + 4y = 9 \quad (1) \\ 3x - 5y = 8 \quad (2) \end{cases}$

We can't use addition or subtraction of two linear equations to eliminate either quantity.

So let's make the coefficients of the two unknowns in these two equations equal or opposite.

Solution   By multiplying (1) × 5 and (2) × 4, we get: $\begin{cases} 10x + 20y = 45 \quad (3) \\ 12x - 20y = 32 \quad (4) \end{cases}$

By adding (3) + (4), we get: $22x = 77$

This gives the solution: $x = \dfrac{7}{2}$

Substitute $x = \dfrac{7}{2}$ into (1) to give: $2 \times \dfrac{7}{2} + 4y = 9$

This gives the solution: $y = \dfrac{1}{2}$

So the solutions to the original system of linear equations are: $\begin{cases} x = \dfrac{7}{2} \\ y = \dfrac{1}{2} \end{cases}$

75

Practice 6.9 (2)

Solve the equations.

a. $\begin{cases} x - 3y = 26 \\ 2x + 3y = -5 \end{cases}$

b. $\begin{cases} 9x - 3y = 16 \\ 9x + 11y = -12 \end{cases}$

c. $\begin{cases} 5x - 3y = 12 \\ 3x + 4y = -8 \end{cases}$

6.10 Solving systems of linear equations with three variables

> If a system of equations contains three unknowns and the power of each variable is 1, then it is known as a **system of linear equations with three variables**.

For example, systems of equations such as

$$\begin{cases} 15x - 3y + 2z = 1 \\ 3x + 4y - z = 18 \\ z = 13 \end{cases} \quad \text{or} \quad \begin{cases} 6x - y - z = 3 \\ 2x - 4y + 8z = 5 \\ 3x - 6y - z = 10 \end{cases}$$

are systems of linear equations with three variables.

How can we solve a system of linear equations with three variables?

Can we solve a system of linear equations with three variables by using elimination?

The method of solving a system of linear equations with three variables is:

system of linear equations with three variables → *elimination* → system of linear equations with two variables → *elimination* → system of linear equations with one variable

Example 1 Solve this system of equations. $\begin{cases} x = 3 & (1) \\ x + y = 5 & (2) \\ 2x + z = 16 & (3) \end{cases}$

Solution

Substitute (1) into (2) to get the solution $y = 2$

Substitute (1) into (3) to get the solution $z = 10$

The solutions to the original system of linear equations are: $\begin{cases} x = 3 \\ y = 2 \\ z = 10 \end{cases}$

Example 2 Solve this system of equations.

$$\begin{cases} 3x + 2y + 5z = 2 & (1) \\ x - 2y - z = 6 & (2) \\ 4x + 2y - 7z = 30 & (3) \end{cases}$$

Which unknown number should be eliminated first?

Analysis The coefficients of the unknown y are equal or opposite in all three equations, so we can add together equations (1) and (2), and equations (2) and (3) to eliminate y. This gives a system of linear equations with two variables: x and z.

Solution

By (1) + (2): $4x + 4z = 8$

Which simplifies to: $x + z = 2$ (4)

By (2) + (3): $5x - 8z = 36$ (5)

By (4) × 5 – (5): $13z = -26$

To give the solution: $z = -2$

Substitute $z = -2$ into (4) to give the solution: $x = 4$

Substitute $x = 4$ and $z = -2$ into (1) to give: $3 \times 4 + 2y + 5 \times (-2) = 2$

to give the solution: $y = 0$

The solutions to the original system of linear equations are: $\begin{cases} x = 4 \\ y = 0 \\ z = -2 \end{cases}$

Example 3 Solve this system of equations.

$\begin{cases} x + y = -14 \ (1) \\ y + z = -7 \ (2) \\ x + z = 19 \ (3) \end{cases}$

← We can also add these three equations together to get $2(x + y + z) = -2$, $x + y + z = -1$ (5). By subtracting (5) – (1), (5) –(2), and (5) – (3), we can get the values of x, y and z, respectively.

Solution

By (1) – (2): $x - z = -7$ (4)

By (3) + (4): $2x = 12$

To give the solution: $x = 6$

Substitute $x = 6$ into (1) to give the solution: $y = -20$

Substitute $x = 6$ into (3) to give the solution: $z = 13$

The solutions to the original system of linear equations are: $\begin{cases} x = 6 \\ y = -20 \\ z = 13 \end{cases}$

Practice 6.10

1. **Which of these systems of equations are systems of linear equations with three variables?**

   a. $\begin{cases} 11x - 3y + 6z = 1 \\ 2x + 4y = 7z \\ 9y - 3z = 0 \end{cases}$

   b. $\begin{cases} 4x - y + 5z = 2 \\ 5x + 6yz = -8 \\ 2x - 7y = 15 \end{cases}$

   c. $\begin{cases} \dfrac{8}{9}x - \dfrac{5}{9}y + 2z = \dfrac{2}{3} \\ 3y - 9x + 18z = -5 \end{cases}$

2. **Solve the equations.**

   a. $\begin{cases} x = 5 \\ x + 5y - 2z = -4 \\ 4x - 3y + 2z = 1 \end{cases}$

   b. $\begin{cases} 9x - 5y + z = -6 \\ 9x + y + 4z = 3 \\ -9x + 3y - 5z = 0 \end{cases}$

   c. $\begin{cases} x + y = 22 \\ x + z = -27 \\ y + z = 13 \end{cases}$

6.11 Applying systems of linear equations

Think!

Tickets for a pop concert at the arena cost £60 for adults and £45 for children. The arena has sold a total of ten thousand tickets. The income for the tickets was £510 000. How many tickets were sold for adults and how many for children?

Analysis   We can write two equations from the question:

Adult tickets + child tickets = 10 000 (1)

60 × the number of adult tickets + 45 × the number of child tickets = 510 000 (2)

Solution   If we set the number of adult tickets as y and child tickets as x, by combining equations (1) and (2) we can solve it as a system of linear equations with two variables:

$$\begin{cases} x + y = 10\,000 \\ 60x + 45y = 510\,000 \end{cases}$$

The method is to set two unknowns, x and y, and write a system of linear equations with two variables, x and y.

When we solve a problem using equations, the number of unknowns should be identified. A system of linear equations with two variables is generally used to solve a problem with two unknowns and a system of linear equations with three variables is generally used to solve a problem with three variables.

Example 1 Class 1 and Class 2 in Year 6 each have 44 pupils and in both classes some pupils have joined the astronomy club. The number of pupils from Class 1 in the astronomy club happens to be one third of the number of pupils from Class 2 not in it. The number of pupils in Class 2 in the astronomy club happens to be one quarter

of the number of pupils in Class 1 not in it. How many pupils from Classes 1 and 2 are not in the astronomy club?

Analysis We can write two equations from the question:

The number of Class 1 pupils in the astronomy club = $\frac{1}{3}$ × the number of Class 2 pupils not in it.

The number of Class 2 pupils in the astronomy club = $\frac{1}{4}$ × the number of Class 1 pupils not in it.

Solution We can set the numbers of pupils from Class 1 and Class 2 who are not in the astronomy club as x and y, respectively. From here we can write the equations:

$$\begin{cases} 44 - x = \frac{1}{3}y \ (1) \\ 44 - y = \frac{1}{4}x \ (2) \end{cases}$$

Rearranging (1) gives: $x = 44 - \frac{1}{3}y$ (3)

Substitute (3) into (2) to give the solution: $y = 36$

Substitute $y = 36$ into (3) to give the solution: $x = 32$

The solutions to this system of linear equations are: $\begin{cases} x = 32 \\ y = 36 \end{cases}$

So 32 pupils in Class 1 and 36 pupils in Class 2 are not in the astronomy club.

✓ Practice 6.11 (1)

1. Mr Khan paid £100 for notebooks and pens as class prizes. There were 22 prizes. If the price of each notebook was £2.50 and the price of each pen was £7, how many notebooks and pens could Mr Khan buy?

2. There are nine carpenters in a workshop making school desks and chairs. Each carpenter can assemble four double desks or ten single chairs per day. How should they plan their daily work so that the number of chairs suits the number of double desks?

3. There are two oil drums, A and B. Drum A contains 400 litres of oil and drum B contains 150 litres of oil. The ratio for the quantities of oil released from the two drums is 2 : 1, and the amount of oil remaining in drum A is four times that remaining in drum B. How many litres of oil are released by each of the drums?

Example 2   The problem at the very beginning of this unit was about how Dylan's household uses a variable rate meter. The unit price of electricity in off-peak periods is lower than it is at peak periods by 31p. This month, the electricity consumption was 127 kilowatt hours during off-peak periods and 283 kilowatt hours during peak periods. The electricity bill comes to £210.73. Find the price of electricity per kilowatt hour during peak periods and off-peak periods.

Analysis   We can complete this table from the question.

	Electricity (kWh)	Unit price (pounds)	Total price (pounds)
Peak periods	283	x	$283x$
Off-peak periods	127	y	$127y$

By setting up two unknown quantities as the unit prices for the two rates we can come up with two write equations.

Solution   We can set x as the unit price during peak periods and y as the unit price during off-peak periods. From here we can write this system of equations:

$$\begin{cases} x - y = 0.31 \\ 283x + 127y = 210.73 \end{cases}$$

The solutions to this system of linear equations are: $\begin{cases} x = 0.61 \\ y = 0.30 \end{cases}$

So the price per kilowatt hour is £0.61 during peak periods and £0.30 during off-peak periods.

Example 3   A basketball player scored 20 points in 10 of his 15 shots and free throws in a game. The number of two-point shots was three times the number of three-point shots. How many three-point shots, two-point shots and free throws, respectively, did the basketball player take in those 10 shots?

Analysis   We must read the question carefully and decide what information we need to solve the problem. In this case, the fact that the basketball player took a total of 15 shots is extra information, which we can ignore.

Solution   Set the number of three-point shots that the basketball player shot as x, the number of two-point shots as y and the number of free throws as z. This leads to the following system of equations:

$$\begin{cases} 3x + 2y + z = 20 \\ x + y + z = 10 \\ y = 3x \end{cases}$$

Can you set up a system of linear equations with two variables to solve this problem?

The solutions to this system of linear equations are: $\begin{cases} y = 6 \\ z = 2 \end{cases}$

So the basketball player took 2 three-point shots, 6 two-point shots and 2 free throws in this game.

Practice 6.11 (2)

Some Year 6 pupils took part in a tree planting activity. They planted a total of 900 willow saplings, Indus saplings and pine saplings. The number of Indus saplings was twice the number of pine saplings and the number of willow saplings was three times the number of Indus saplings. How many willow saplings, Indus saplings and pine saplings, respectively, did they plant?

Unit summary

In this unit you have learned about writing and solving: linear equations with one variable; linear equations with two variables (including systems of linear equations with two variables); systems of linear equations with three variables; and linear inequalities with one variable (including systems of linear inequalities with one variable). When you study, you should pay attention to the similarities and differences between equations and inequalities and their solutions. You should understand and use methods of elimination and transformation. You should also regularly practise solving practical problems with equations.

Awareness of the following three aspects can help you to get the most out of this unit:

1. Writing and solving equations and inequalities; their similarities and their differences

2. Methods for transforming equations and inequalities

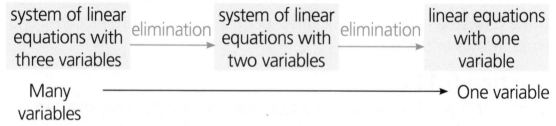

3. How problems, equations and solutions relate to each other

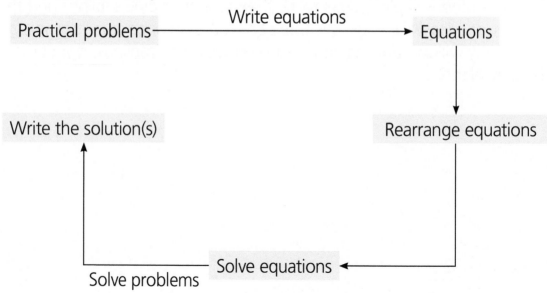

Investigation activity: Route problem investigation

Dylan and Emma stand at vertices D and C of a square field with sides of 12 metres ($ABCD$). They begin walking in a clockwise direction around its perimeter. Dylan walks at a speed of 1 metre per second and Emma at 1.2 metres per second.

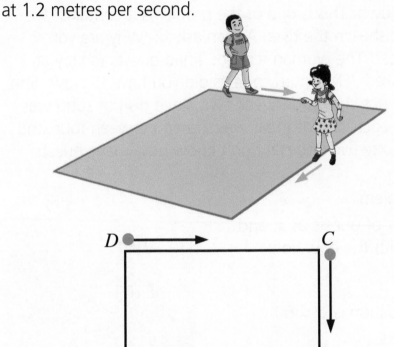

1. After how many seconds do Dylan and Emma return to their initial positions at vertices D and C for the first time? After how many seconds do Dylan and Emma arrive at vertices D and C for the second time? What is the rule?

2. After how many seconds do Dylan and Emma arrive at a new vertex of the square for the first time? What is the rule?

3. After how many seconds do Dylan and Emma arrive at the same vertex of the square for the first time? What is the rule?

4. Is it possible for Dylan and Emma to arrive at vertex D at the same time? How? Is it possible for Dylan to arrive at vertex D at the same time that Emma arrives at vertex B?

Extra reading material: Two examples of ancient Chinese equations

Example 1

Sunzi's Mathematical Classic is a mathematical work written around 400 years BC in ancient China. It was not actually written by the Sunzi and the author is unknown. This is one of the problems it contains: A woman was washing dishes in the river. A man asked: 'Why are you washing so many dishes?' The woman replied: 'I had guests to stay at my home.' The man asked: 'How many guests did you have to stay?' She said: 'Each dish of rice was shared between two, each dish of soup was shared between three, each dish of meat was shared between four, and they shared a total of sixty-five dishes. I don't know how many guests there were.'

Can you solve this problem?

We can set the number of guests as x, and from there come up with the equation:

$$\frac{x}{2} + \frac{x}{3} + \frac{x}{4} = 65$$

The solution to the equation is: $x = 60$

So there were 60 guests.

Example 2

This is a problem from *The Nine Chapters on the Mathematical Art*, an ancient Chinese book of mathematical problems: There are five sheep, four dogs, three chickens and two rabbits. Together they are worth 1496 Qian. Four sheep, two dogs, six chickens and three rabbits are worth 1175 Qian. Three sheep, a dog, seven chickens and five rabbits are worth 958 Qian. Two sheep, three dogs, five chickens and a rabbit are worth 861 Qian. How much is each sheep, dog, chicken and rabbit worth?

A sheep is worth 177 Qian, a dog is worth 120 Qian, a chicken is worth 23 Qian and a rabbit is worth 29 Qian. This is a problem that involves solving a system of linear equations with four variables. Use the maths that you have learned in this unit to check whether the ancient answer is correct.

The examples above show that the ancient Chinese had knowledge of equations. They would arrange systems of equations into square arrays and then solve them by moving counting rods, which is different from the method we use to solve equations today.

Unit Seven: Constructing line segments and angles

Plans and designs for many everyday objects, machine parts, buildings and other structures are based on basic geometric elements such as line segments and angles.

In this unit you will learn about the simplest of these geometric elements – line segments and angles. You will compare them and learn how to construct them. You will use measuring tools such as rulers, protractors and compasses. You will learn how to construct a line segment of the same length as a given line segment and to construct an angle that is the same size as a given angle. If you can construct line segments and angles, you can research and construct other more complicated geometric shapes, such as triangles and quadrilaterals.

Section One: The equivalence, sum, difference and scalar multiples of line segments

7.1 Comparing the lengths of line segments

💡 Think!

How can we represent a line segment?

We can use uppercase letters to represent two endpoints of a line segment. As shown in the diagram below, a line segment can be represented by the letters A and B, used to identify its endpoints. This is written as: 'line segment AB.'

As shown in the diagram, it is also possible to use a lowercase letter such as 'a' to represent a line segment. This is written as: 'line segment a.'

A ———————————— B
   ——————— a

❓ Problem

Are the two pencils in the picture as long as each other? Which one is longer? How can you compare them?

We can use a ruler to measure these two pencils. After measuring we can compare their lengths.

A simpler method is shown in the diagram: we can move them next to each other and align them at one end. This way we can compare their lengths directly.

If we regard these two pencils as line segments, we can rewrite the question above to use more technical language. Generally, we refer to comparing the length of two line segments as a **comparison of the length of line segments**.

This diagram shows the basic method for the comparison of the length of line segments.

Think!

If we move line segment *AB* to the position of line segment *CD*, aligning endpoint *A* with endpoint *C* and superimposing line segment *AB* onto line segment *CD*, how many possible positions are there for endpoint *B*?

	Diagram	The position of endpoint *B*	Symbolic representation
Case 1	*A* *B* (*A*) (*B*) *C* *D*	Endpoint *B* is on line segment *CD* (between endpoint *C* and endpoint *D*)	This is written as $AB < CD$ (or $CD > AB$)
Case 2	*A* *B* (*A*) (*B*) *C* *D*	Endpoint *B* aligns with endpoint *D*	This is written as $AB = CD$
Case 3	*A* *B* (*A*) (*B*) *C* *D*	Endpoint *B* is on the extension of line segment *CD*	This is written as $AB > CD$ (or $CD < AB$)

Example 1 Line segment *a* is shown below. Use a pair of compasses and a ruler to construct a line segment *AB* equal to line segment *a*.

a

Solution 1. Construct a ray *AC*.

2. Open the compasses so that the distance between the point and the pencil tip is the same as the length of *a*. Put the point of the compasses on the endpoint *A* and draw an arc ← that passes through *AC*. Mark the point where it cuts *AC* as *B*.

Line segment *AB* is the line segment we want to construct.

Taking point *A* as the centre of the circle, construct an arc with radius equal to the length of *a*, then the arc intersects the ray *AC* at point *B*.

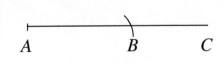

a

A   *B*   *C*

Example 2 First observe and estimate the lengths of line segment a and line segment b below, then compare them.

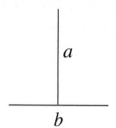

I estimate that $b < a$!

Solution 1. Construct a ray OC.

2. With the compasses set to the length of a and the point on endpoint O, draw an arc that crosses OC. Mark this as point A. With the compasses set to the length of b and the point on endpoint O, draw an arc that crosses OC. Mark this as point B.

Because point B is on the extension of line segment OA, so B is further away from O than A is, $OA < OB$, which means that $a < b$. The distance between the two endpoints of a line is the length of the line segment. We can use this fact to compare the lengths of a and b. The line segment connecting the endpoints A and B is equivalent to the difference between the lengths of a and b.

It seems that observation and estimation are not necessarily reliable!

> The length of a line segment connecting two points is called the **distance** between the two points.

Think!

There are three paths between attractions A and B in a park, as shown in the diagram below. Emma wants to go from attraction A to attraction B as quickly as possible. Help her to choose the path. Why did you choose it?

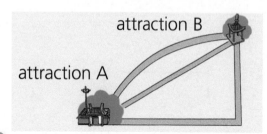

attraction B

attraction A

Tell us the reason why you chose this path. How can you prove this path is the shortest?

Summary

The shortest distance between two points is a straight line segment.

 ## Practice 7.1

1. Compare the length of the line segments *AB* and *CD* in each of the figures below.

2. *AB* and *CD* and are two line segments, and *AB* > *CD*. If we move line segment *CD* to lie on top of line segment *AB*, aligning endpoints *C* and *A* so that line segment *CD* is along line segment *AB*, what is the position of endpoint *D*, in relation to endpoint *B*?

3. Use a ruler to measure the distance between point *A* and point *B* (to the nearest whole millimetre).

A

B

7.2 Constructing the sum, difference and scalar multiples of line segments

Think!

We know that rational numbers can be added and subtracted. Can line segments, as geometric shapes, be added and subtracted?

Yes, they can.

Observation

Points *A*, *B* and *C* are in a straight line, as shown in the diagram on the right.

$A \quad B \quad C$

1. How many line segments are there in the picture?

2. What are the relationships between these line segments?

There are three line segments: *AB*, *BC* and *AC*. They have the following relationships:

$$AB + BC = AC \quad AC - BC = AB \quad AC - AB = BC$$

> Two line segments can be added (or subtracted). Their sum (or difference) is also a line segment and its length is equal to the sum (or difference) of the length of the two line segments.

Example 1* Line segment *a* and line segment *b* are shown in the diagram on the right.

a. Construct a line segment and make its length equal to the length of *a* + *b*.

a

b. Construct a line segment and make its length equal to the length of *a* − *b*.

b

Solution

a.

1. Construct a ray *OP*.

2. With the compasses set to the length of *a*, and the point on endpoint *O*, draw an arc to cut *OP*. Label the point where the arc cuts the line as *A*. With the compasses set to the length of *b*, and the point on *A*, draw an arc on *AP*. Label the point where the arc cuts the line as *B*. The line segment *OB* is the line segment we want to construct.

b.

1. Construct a ray *OP*.

2. Cut the line segment *OC* = *a* on the ray *OP*. Cut the line segment *CD* = *b* on the ray *CO*.

The line segment *OD* is the line segment we want to construct.

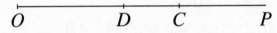

 # Think!

We multiply line segment *a* by a positive integer *n* and write it down as *na* (*n* > 1 and *n* is a positive integer). What does *na* mean?

> This is the same operation as when we multiply 5 by 4, which means adding 5 fours together. *na* means we add together *n* line segments *a*. Of course, *na* can also be interpreted as *n* times the length of line segment *a*.

Example 2* Line segment *a* and line segment *b* are shown in the diagram on the right.

Construct a line segment that is equal to 2*a* – *b*.

Analysis Regard 2*a* as *a* + *a*.

 Try to complete this example by yourself.

> The point that cuts a line segment into two equal line segments is called the **midpoint** of the line segment.

Point M is the midpoint of line segment AB, as shown on the right. Five ways of representing this are:

$$AM = BM,$$
$$AM = \frac{1}{2}AB,\ MB = \frac{1}{2}AB$$
$$AB = 2AM,\ AB = 2MB$$

Example 3* Given line segment AB, construct its midpoint, C.

Solution

a. Use a ruler to confirm that $AB = 5$ centimetres.

b. Mark line segment $AC = 2.5$ centimetres on line segment AB. Point C is the midpoint of line segment AB.

Example 4* Given line segment AB, use a ruler and a pair of compasses to construct its midpoint, C.

Solution

a. Open the compasses to a radius that is greater than half the length of line segment AB. With the compass point on A, construct an arc as shown, curving above and below line segment AB and cutting it at D. Keeping the compasses set to the same radius, and with the point on B, construct a second arc, curving above and below line segment AB and cutting it at E. Label the points where the arcs cross as F and G.

b. Construct the line segment FG. It intersects line segment AB at point C. Point C is the midpoint of line segment AB.

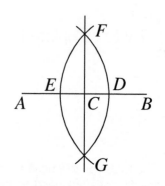

*Example 3 is a measurement construction while Example 4 is a construction with ruler and compasses. You will learn the principles of the method of construction in Example 4 later on.

Practice 7.2

1. **Look at the diagram on the right and fill in the blanks.**

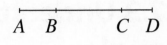

   a. $AB + BC = ($ $)$
   b. $AD = ($ $) + CD$
   c. $CD = AD - ($ $)$
   d. $BD = CD + ($ $) = AD - ($ $)$
   e. $AC - AB + CD = ($ $) = BC + ($ $)$

2. **In the line segment AB shown in the diagram below, point C is the midpoint of line segment AD, $AC = 1\frac{1}{2}$ cm and $BC = 2\frac{1}{5}$ cm.**

   a. $AD = ($ $)$ cm
   b. $BD = ($ $)$ cm

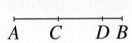

3. **The diagram shows line segments a and b, where $a > 2b$.**

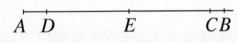

   Fill in the blanks to describe how to construct a line segment and make its length equal to the length of $a - 2b$.

   a. Construct a ray (   ).
   b. Mark the line segment (   ) $= a$ on the ray (   ).
   c. Mark the line segment (   ) $= b$ and the line segment (   ) $= b$ in order on the line segment (   ).
   Line segment (   ) is the line segment you want to construct.

4. **Use a ruler and a pair of compasses to bisect the line segment AB.**

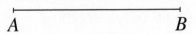

Section Two: Angles
7.3 Understanding and representing angles

Angles are formed between two rays with a common endpoint. As shown in the diagram to the right, the common endpoint is called the **vertex** of the angle and the two lines are called the **rays** of the angle.

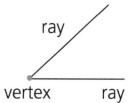

ray

vertex   ray

 # Observation

If you close up the arms of a pair of compasses and lay it flat on a table, this could be considered as a single ray extending from an axis. Then, if you rotate one of the arms to open up the compasses, what shape does the rotated arm and the non-rotated arm form?

This is another way to describe the idea of an angle.

An angle is a shape that is formed by a ray rotating to another position around its endpoint. As shown in the diagram on the right, the ray that is in the initial position is called the **initial side** of the angle and the ray that is in the terminal position is called the **terminal side** of the angle.

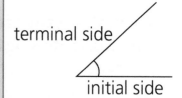

terminal side

initial side

The smaller angle between the initial and terminal sides of the angle is usually called the **interior angle**. The interior angle can be indicated with an arc or an arrow. We can also use an arc to mark the angle between the terminal side and the initial side of the angle, on the 'outside'. This is called the **exterior** angle.

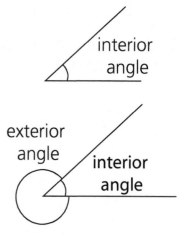

interior angle

exterior angle

interior angle

If there is no indication of whether a question refers to the interior or exterior angle, the questions in this book will be referring to the interior (acute) angle.

We often use three uppercase letters← to represent angles. As shown in the left-hand diagram below, this is written in the format ∠AOB.

> The uppercase letter 'O', which represents the vertex of the angle, always comes in the middle of the three uppercase letters.

If a vertex is identified by an uppercase letter, we can use that single letter to represent an angle, provided that it is clear exactly which angle we mean. In the left-hand diagram below, ∠AOB can be written as ∠O. To avoid confusion, if there are several angles meeting at the same vertex represented by the same letter (as shown at vertex O in the centre diagram below), they should all be identified by three uppercase letters.

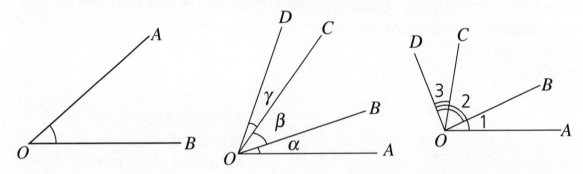

Sometimes, for convenience, we mark the interior of an angle using a lowercase letter, such as a or b, or a Greek letter such as α (alpha), β (beta) or γ (gamma). As shown in the centre diagram above, ∠AOB, ∠BOC, ∠COD can be written as ∠α, ∠β and ∠γ (or α, β, γ), respectively. As shown in the right-hand diagram above, we can also use numbers, such as 1, 2 and 3, so ∠AOB, ∠BOC, ∠COD can be written as ∠1, ∠2 and ∠3, respectively.

Example   To get to Zhenru Town, you leave People's Square on the road heading west, but have to turn through 30° northwards. Alternatively, you could describe the direction as 60° west of the north line that runs through People's Square.

In the diagram, the line *ON* represents the north line from point *O* (People's Square). The line *OE* runs east, the line *OS* runs south and the line *OW* runs west from point *O*.

Using point *O* to represent People's Square and point *B* to represent Zhenru Town, construct a line from People's Square to Zhenru Town.

How would you describe the line *OA*?

Solution   We can regard point *O* as the vertex of the angle and the ray *ON* as the first side. From here we can construct $\angle NOB = 60°$ within the right angle $\angle NOW$. The line *OB* shows the direction from People's Square to Zhenru Town. (It represents the direction that is 60 degrees west of north.)

> The line *OA* runs 30° east of north.

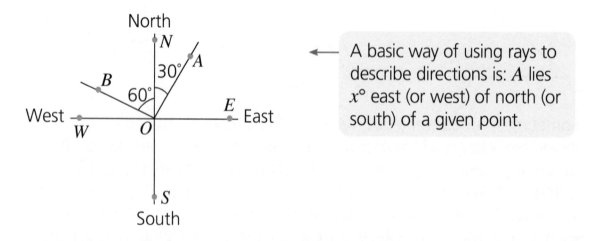

> A basic way of using rays to describe directions is: *A* lies *x*° east (or west) of north (or south) of a given point.

Practice 7.3

1. **Mark letters onto the angles below, write the notation for each angle and point out the vertex and rays of each angle.**

2. **Write the vertex and the rays of $\angle ABC$, $\angle POQ$ and $\angle XYZ$.**

3. Look at the diagrams and the descriptions below. Describe any mistakes and correct them.

a.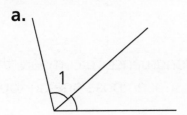

This is written as: ∠ABC

b.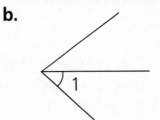

This is written as: ∠B

Solution

a. The mistake is _____. It should be written as _____.

b. The mistake is _____. It should be written as _____.

4. The angle marked 1 in each diagram is the interior angle. Draw an angle arc to show the exterior angle in each diagram.

a.

b.

7.4 Constructing and comparing the sizes of angles

? Problem

How can we compare the sizes of angles?

To compare the lengths of line segments we use the methods of measurement and congruence, so I think we can use the same methods to compare the size of angles.

 Can we use the protractor to measure them?

 If two objects are exactly the same shape and exactly the same size, even if one is the mirror image of the other, they are **congruent**.

Can we use the method of congruence to compare the sizes of angles? How can we superimpose one on top of the other?

✎ Try it out!

Use a protractor to measure the angles ∠ABC and ∠DEF, then compare their sizes.

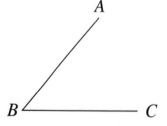

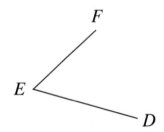

We can use a method similar to the method of superimposing line segments. Move an angle; superimpose its vertex and the vertex of the other angle; superimpose one of its rays onto one of the rays of the other angle. The other (terminal) side of the two angles should be on the same side of the superimposed rays. This way, we can compare their sizes by eye.

Think!

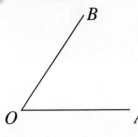

The angle ∠AOB is shown on the left. If we copy ∠DEF, matching vertices O and E and matching lines ED and OA, do the lines EF and OB also match? What are the possible relationships between line EF and ∠AOB? Write the missing information into the table (you might want to refer to the table in Unit 7, Section 1).

	Diagram	Relationship between Line EF and ∠AOB	Symbolic representation
Case 1	B, F O (E) A (D)	Line EF lies within ∠AOB	∠DEF < ∠AOB (or ∠AOB > ∠DEF)
Case 2	B (F) O (E) A (D)		
Case 3	F B O (E) A (D)		

Example 1 The diagram shows ∠α is known. Use a protractor to construct ∠AOB, where ∠AOB = ∠α.

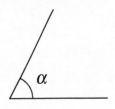

Solution

1. By measuring with a protractor, we find that $\angle \alpha = 65°$.

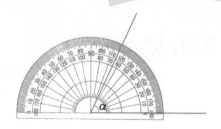

2. Now construct $\angle AOB = 65°$
$\angle AOB$ is the angle we want to construct.

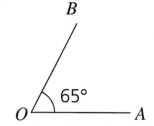

Example 2 The diagram shows $\angle \beta$. Use a ruler and a pair of compasses to construct $\angle COD$, where $\angle COD = \angle \beta$.

Solution

1. Construct a ray OC.

2. Set your compasses to a suitable radius, a, and place the compass point on the vertex of β. Draw an arc to cut the arms of β at E and F respectively.

3. Keeping the compasses as set, with radius a, place the compass point on point O and draw an arc intersecting ray OC at point M (as shown in the diagram below).

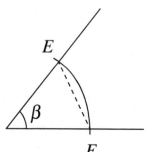

4. Set your compasses to a radius equal to the length of EF. Place your compass point on the point M and draw an arc to intersect the previous arc at point N.

5. Construct ray OD through points O and N.

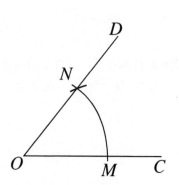

Think!

Look at the diagram. Fill in the missing information and circle the correct answers.

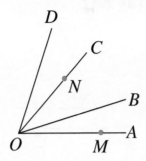

1. Compare the sizes of angles.

   ∠*BOC* and ∠*BOD* share a common edge, ray *OB*. Line (*OA* / *OC*) lies within ∠*BOD*, so ∠*BOC* (< / > / =) ∠*BOD*.

   ∠*AOB* and ∠*AOC* share a (   ), ray *OA*. Ray *OC* lies (within / outside) ∠*AOB*, so ∠*AOC* (< / > / =) ∠*AOB*.

2. Find the edges of angles.

   Ray *OC* is the common edge to ∠*BOC* and ∠*AOC*.

   ∠*BOC* < ∠*AOC*, so ray *OA* lies (within / outside) ∠*BOC*.

   Line *OM* is congruent to ray (   ). ∠*MON* = ∠*AOC*, so line *ON* and ray (   ) are (   ).

Practice 7.4

1. **Compare the angles in each pair and write <, = or > in each space.**

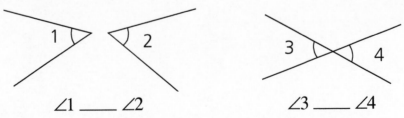

∠1 _____ ∠2   ∠3 _____ ∠4

2. **Use a protractor to construct ∠*AOB* = 125°. Construct ∠*BOC* = 55° outside ∠*AOB*, with the two angles sharing ray *OB*. What do you notice about rays *OA* and *OC*?**

3. Line BC and $\angle\alpha$ are shown below. Use a ruler and a pair of compasses to construct $\angle ABC$. Make $\angle ABC = \angle\alpha$ (there is no need to show your construction method). How many possible positions are there for ray BA?

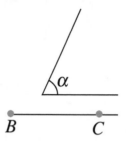

4. Look at the diagrams below and fill in the brackets.

Copy $\angle AOB$ over $\angle MPN$. Make point O and point ( ) congruent. Line OA lies over line ( ).

OB and PN are on the same side of PM.

$\angle AOB = \angle MPN$, so line OB lies over line ( ).

Line $OB = $ line PN, so point ( ) and point ( ) are congruent.

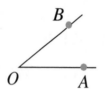 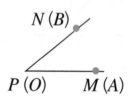

7.5 Constructing the sum, difference and scalar multiples of angles

? Problem

Line segments can be added and subtracted. Can angles be added or subtracted? If so, can we use a similar method to that used for line segments?

◦ Observation

As shown in the diagram here, the ray OC lies within $\angle AOB$. How many angles can you find in the diagram? Are there any relationships between any of their sizes?

There are 3 angles in total: $\angle AOC$, $\angle COB$ and $\angle AOB$. The relationships between their sizes are:

$$\angle AOC + \angle COB = \angle AOB$$
$$\angle AOB - \angle AOC = \angle COB$$
$$\angle AOB - \angle COB = \angle AOC$$

Summary

> Two angles can be added (or subtracted). Their sum (or difference) is also an angle. The size of this angle is equal to the sum (or difference) of the sizes of the original two angles.

Try it out!

Use a pair of set squares to construct two angles, 75° and 15°.

You can use a pair of set squares to construct 30°, 45°, 60° and 90°. You can construct angles of 75° and 15° by using the sum and difference of these angles (as shown on the right).

Think: Which other angles can be constructed with a pair of set squares?

Example 1 You are given $\angle \alpha$ and $\angle \beta$ (as shown below). Use a protractor to construct an angle that is equal to $\angle \alpha + \angle \beta$.

15°   75°

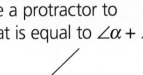 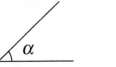

Analysis We know how to use a protractor to construct an angle that is equal to a known angle. We can construct an angle that is equal to $\angle\alpha$ + $\angle\beta$ by adding the angles together.

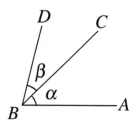

Solution

1. Use a protractor to construct $\angle ABC = \angle\alpha$.

2. Use a protractor to construct $\angle CBD = \angle\beta$ next to $\angle ABC$ with the vertex of $\angle\beta$ at the centre of the protractor and ray BC along the base line. $\angle ABC$ is the angle we want to construct.

 ## Think!

Do you remember what the midpoint of a line segment is? It's the point that divides a line segment into two equal parts. Is there a line that divides an angle into two equal parts?

 ## Try it out!

Cut out a triangle of any size from a piece of paper. Carefully fold the paper triangle so that two of its edges align, then open it up again. What can you see?

Divide the angle into two equal angles.

If a ray from the vertex of an angle divides the angle into two equal parts, then the ray is known as an **angle bisector**.

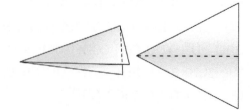

As shown on the right, OC is the angle bisector of $\angle AOB$. Another way of saying this is that OC halves $\angle AOB$.

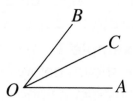

$\angle AOC = \angle BOC = \dfrac{1}{2}\angle AOB$

Or $\angle AOB = 2\angle AOC = 2\angle BOC$

Example 2 You are given ∠*ABC* as shown on the right. Construct its angle bisector.

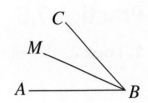

Solution

1. Use a protractor to measure ∠*ABC* = 48°.

2. Construct a ray *BM* within ∠*ABC* so that
   ∠*ABM* = 24°.
   BM is the angle bisector of ∠*ABC*.

 Think!

You have learned to use a protractor and a ruler to construct an angle bisector of a known angle. Can you construct an angle bisector of a known angle using only a pair of compasses and ruler?

Example 3 ∠*ABC* is known (as shown in the diagram below). Construct *OC*, the angle bisector of ∠*AOB*.

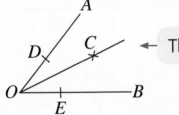 ← This shows the construction of an angle bisector.

Solution

1. Using compasses, with the point on *O*, draw arcs of equal radius on lines *OA* and *OB*. Mark the points as *D* and *E*, respectively.

2. Using compasses, with the point on *D*, construct an arc inside ∠*AOB*. Keep the compasses at the same width and repeat with the point of the compasses on *E*. The two arcs will intersect at *C*.

3. Construct a ray *OC*. *OC* is the angle bisector of ∠*AOB*.

Example 4 In the diagram, ∠1 = ∠3 = *m*° and ∠2 = *n*°.

a. Use an equation containing *m* and *n* to express the sizes of angles ∠*AOC* and ∠*BOD*.

b. Compare the sizes of ∠*AOC* and ∠*BOD*.

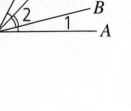

Solution

a. ∠1 = ∠3 = *m*° and ∠2 = *n*°, so

Size of ∠*AOC* = size of ∠1 + size of ∠2 = *m* + *n*

Size of ∠*BOD* = size of ∠2 + size of ∠3 = *n* + *m*

b. Size of ∠*AOC* is equal to size of ∠*BOD*, so ∠*AOC* = ∠*BOD*

✏ Practice 7.5

1. Look at the diagrams and fill in the brackets.

a. In the diagram, ∠AOB = ∠BOC = ∠COD,

so ∠AOD = ∠AOC + (   )

            = (   ) + ∠BOD

            = (   ) + ∠BOC + (   )

            = 3 (   )

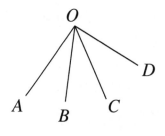

b. In the diagram, ∠AOD = 80° and ∠COD = 30°.

OB is the angle bisector of ∠AOC,

so ∠AOC = (   )° and ∠AOB = (   )°.

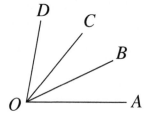

2. In the diagram, ∠AOB = 62°, ∠1 = (3x − 2)° and ∠2 = (x + 8)°. Find the sizes of ∠1 and ∠2 in degrees.

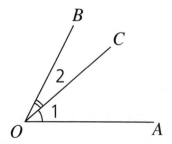

3. a. The diagram shows ∠α and ∠β. Use a ruler and protractor to construct ∠DEF = 2∠α − ∠β.

b. Now construct ∠MON = 3∠α.

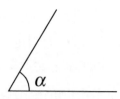

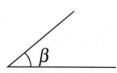

4. The diagram shows ∠A and ∠B. Construct the angle bisectors of ∠A and ∠B and their point of intersection, O.

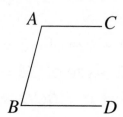

7.6 Complementary and supplementary angles

Try it out!

Measure the sizes of ∠α, ∠β and ∠γ. Think about the relationships between the sizes of the two pairs of angles, ∠α and ∠β, and ∠β and ∠γ. What do you observe?

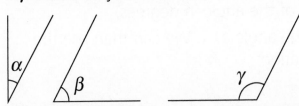

> The sum of ∠α and ∠β is 90° and the sum of ∠β and ∠γ is 180°.

> If the sum of two angles is 90°, the two angles are called **complementary angles**. One is complementary to the other.
> If the sum of two angles is 180°, the two angles are called **supplementary angles**. One is supplementary to the other.

In the diagrams above, ∠α and ∠β are complementary angles. ∠α is complementary to ∠β. ∠β is complementary to ∠α. This can be expressed with the equations:

$∠β = 90° − ∠α, ∠α = 90° − ∠β$

When we look closely at angles, sometimes we need smaller units than degrees. These smaller units are

> How can we show in an equation that ∠β and ∠γ are supplementary angles?

called **minutes and seconds**. If we divide an angle of one degree into 60 equivalent parts, each part is one minute, written as 1'. Then if we divide an angle of one minute into 60 equivalent parts, each part is one second, written as 1".

The relationship between degrees, minutes and seconds (as units of measurement for angles) is:

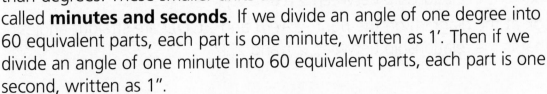

$1° = 60', 1' = 60".$ ← This system is based on units of 60.

Example 1 We know that $\angle\alpha = 53°38'$. Find the complementary and supplementary angles of $\angle\alpha$ in degrees and minutes.

Solution

The complementary angle of $\angle\alpha = 90° - 53°38' = 36°22'.$ ← $90° = 89°60'$

The supplementary angle of $\angle\alpha = 180° - 53°38' = 126°22'.$

Example 2 We are told that the supplementary angle of an angle is three times larger than its complementary angle. Find the size of the angle in degrees.

$180° = 179°60'$

Solution We can set the size of the angle as x. We can then use the question to write the following equation:

$180 - x = 3(90 - x)$

$x = 45$

So the angle is 45°.

💡 Think!

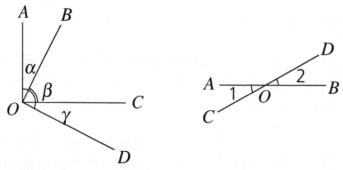

Look at the diagram on the left. $\angle AOC$ and $\angle BOD$ are right angles. What is the relationship between $\angle\alpha$ and $\angle\gamma$?

Look at the diagram on the right. $\angle AOB$ and $\angle COD$ are straight angles. What is the relationship between $\angle1$ and $\angle2$?

Summary

Angles of the same size have equivalent complementary angles.
Angles of the same size have equivalent supplementary angles.

 ## Practice 7.6

1. a. Construct a ray *AB* on the left-hand diagram and make ∠*BAC* and ∠*CAD* complementary angles.

 b. Construct a ray *AE* on the right-hand diagram and make ∠*EAC* and ∠*CAD* supplementary angles.

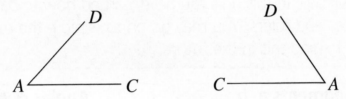

2. a. An angle is equal to its complementary angle. What is the angle?

 b. An angle is equal to its supplementary angle. What is the angle?

 c. Can supplementary angles both be acute? Can they both be right angles? Can they both be obtuse angles?

3. Write the answers to these sums.

 a. 77°54'36" + 34°27'44"   **b.** 89°6'4" − 24°27'35"

4. An angle's supplementary angle is 35° more than two times the size of its complementary angle. What is the size of the angle?

Unit summary

When it comes to comparison, addition and subtraction of angles, and the length of line segments, you can measure them using a protractor and a ruler. You can then compare, add and subtract the quantity you have obtained. This textbook pays more attention to construction using a pair of compasses and a ruler without scales because the method tends to be more direct, exact and straightforward and it involves more advanced rational thinking.

Constructing an exact copy of a known line segment or angle is an important basic skill. In this unit you have learned how to construct one with compasses and rulers. You may go on to explore the mathematical methodology behind this in the future.

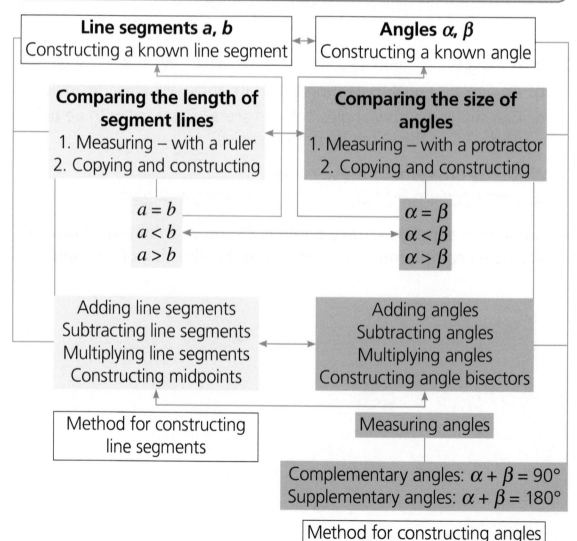

Investigation activity: Shapes formed from line segments

Look at the construction method shown in the first diagram. Then, using the same method, try to complete the other two diagrams on your own.

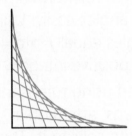  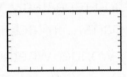

The diagram below shows a circle that contains both of the endpoints for many line segments. Measure the lengths of the line segments. What do you observe? Finish the diagram by constructing your own line segments. Draw as many as possible, but they all have to fit the conditions of the ones already drawn for you. What kind of shapes are formed from these line segments?

Does the diagram you have completed look how you expected? This process is known as curve stitching. The shapes formed from line segments are beautiful curves.

Can you construct any other similar figures?

Extra reading material: Can an angle be trisected using only a ruler and a pair of compasses?

You have learned to construct angle bisectors using a ruler and a pair of compasses. This means that you can halve known angles easily. Using this method repeatedly, you can divide known angles equally into 4 parts, 8 parts… in fact, into 2^n parts (where n is a positive integer).

You may wonder whether an angle can be trisected using rulers and compasses. This question drew many mathematicians' attention in ancient Greece; some spent their lifetime working on solving it. This problem is called the **trisection of an angle**, and it is one of the three famous **questions of construction**.

For thousands of years, mathematicians have thoroughly explored the question of the trisection of an angle. It had great influence on Greek geometry and led to many of the discoveries counted among the highest cultural treasures of the world. However, no answer has been found, despite the study of generations of mathematicians. In the 19th century, more than two thousand years after the question was first proposed, it was finally proved that this construction was impossible using only a ruler and a pair of compasses.

The question was answered through the verification of the **impossibility** of the solution. The goal of **problem solution** was never achieved. However, the various efforts made to solve the problem over more than two thousand years greatly promoted the development of mathematics and the formation of culture and cultural predecessors in society. This example illustrates that fascinating and unsolved problems are an important part of the study of mathematics. In the exploration and solution of an important problem, we should not only pay attention to the result, but also focus on the process. The process may be much more valuable than the solution to the problem itself.

Unit Eight: Recognising cuboids

Could we make the wooden frames in this picture in real life?

8.1 Properties of a cuboid

? Problem

Can you think of any cuboid objects?

How many faces, vertices and edges does a cuboid have?

A cuboid has 6 **faces**, 8 **vertices** and 12 **edges**.

Look at the two cuboids below. What do you notice about the edges and faces that are the same colour?

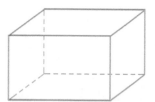
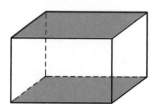

Each side of this cuboid is rectangular.

 Faces that are the same colour are the same shape and size.

The edges of the same colour are the same length.

📝 Summary

A cube is a special kind of cuboid. →

A cuboid may have two square faces. Could a cuboid have four square faces?

1. Each side of the cuboid is a rectangle or a square.
2. The 12 edges of the cuboid can be divided into three groups: each group has 4 edges of equal length.
3. The 6 faces of the cuboid can be divided into three groups: each group has 2 faces of the same size and shape.

Try it out!

Use modelling clay and paper straws to make a cuboid frame that is 6 cm long, 8 cm wide and 10 cm high.

How many straws of each length do we need?

Practice 8.1

1. Give some real-life examples of cuboids.

2. True or false? Put a tick (✓) for 'true' or a cross (✗) for 'false' in the brackets.

   A. All faces of a cuboid are always rectangles. ( )

   B. A cuboid has 12 edges. ( )

   C. A shape with 6 faces, 12 edges and 8 vertices is a cuboid. ( )

   D. The faces on opposite sides of a cuboid are equal. ( )

3. Use sticky tape and cardboard to make a cuboid box.

4. Dylan wants to use a long, thin plastic pipe and modelling clay to make a cuboid box with edges 10 cm, 30 cm and 15 cm in length. He has 250 cm of pipe. Does he have enough? How should he cut it?

8.2 Constructing diagrams of cuboids

Look at the faces of a cuboid. We can see that each face is a flat, 2D shape. Classroom walls, the top of your desk and calm water are also 2D shapes.

A plane is a flat and boundless region. Flat shapes that have only length and width are called 2D or plane shapes. In mathematics, we sometimes need to make 2D drawings of 3D shapes. The sides are often plane shapes, but we can use parallelograms to represent them. We generally use horizontal lines to represent the width, then we draw lines that slope at 45° to represent the edges that are perpendicular to these. The diagram shows horizontal lines representing the length of the top of a cuboid. The sloping lines represent the width. The plane that contains the top of the box may be called 'plane $ABCD$.' We can also write the lowercase Greek letter α at a corner of the parallelogram, and use this to represent the plane. This is written as 'plane α.'

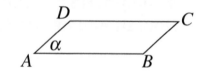

? Problem

Look at the cuboid chalk box and think about how you would draw it.

There are a variety of drawing methods, but we usually use the method described above.

This method is called **oblique secondary auxiliary drawing**.

These are the basic steps for drawing a diagram of a cuboid.
1. Draw a parallelogram *ABCD* so that *AB* is the length of the cuboid and *AD* is equal to one half of the length. ∠*DAB* = 45° (as shown in Figure 1).
2. Draw a vertical line *AE* upwards from point *A*, and a vertical line *BF* upwards from point *B*. Draw a vertical line *CG* upwards from point *C*, and a vertical line *DH* upwards from point *D*. All of these vertical lines should have length equal to the height of the cuboid (as shown in Figure 2).
3. Connect points *E*, *F*, *G* and *H* in sequence (as shown in Figure 3).
4. Change the hidden line segments to dotted or dashed lines (as shown in Figure 4).

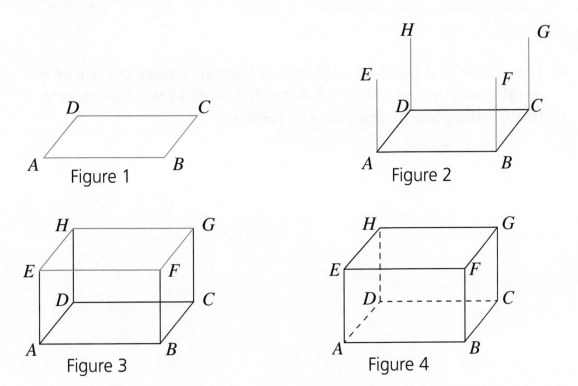

Figure 1

Figure 2

Figure 3

Figure 4

The cuboid shown in Figure 4 is usually described as: cuboid *ABCD-EFGH*. Its 6 faces are usually expressed as: plane *ABCD*, plane *ABFE*, plane *BCGF* and so on. Its 12 edges are usually expressed as: edge *AB*, edge *AE*, edge *EF* and so on.

Practice 8.2

1. Give some real-life examples of planes.

2. Use letters to identify these planes correctly.

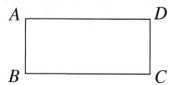 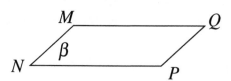

3. Which of these shapes is a cuboid?

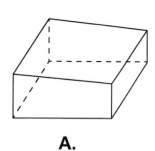 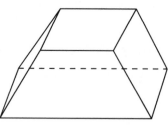 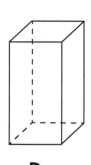

   A.   B.   C.   D.

4. The shape of a piece of rubber is a cuboid. Emma measures its length, width and height as 4 cm, 2 cm and 1 cm, respectively. Draw a diagram of the piece of rubber.

8.3 Understanding the relationships between the edges of a cuboid

In the cuboid *ABCD-EFGH* on the right, edge *EH* is in the same plane as edge *EF* and they have a unique common point. We say that the two edges **intersect**.

Edge *EF* is also in the same plane as edge *AB*, but they do not have a common point. We say that the two edges are **parallel** to each other.

The edges *EH* and *AB* are not parallel and they do not intersect. We say that the two edges are **skew**.

Any two white lines on the running track in the picture are parallel to each other.

The crossbar of the iron gate in the picture intersects with each vertical rail, and any two vertical railings or cross rails are parallel to each other.

The railway tracks and the road in the picture are skew.

In general, if straight line *AB* has a unique common point with straight line *CD*, then we say that line *AB* intersects line *CD*. In general, if straight line *AB* is in the same plane as straight line *CD*, but there is no common point, then we say that line *AB* is parallel to line *CD*. This can be written as: $AB \parallel CD$.

Two straight lines have three possible positional relationships: intersecting, parallel and skew.

In general, if straight line *AB* is neither intersecting with nor parallel to straight line *CD*, then we say that line *AB* and line *CD* are skew.

Example In the cuboid *ABCD-EFGH*:

a. Which edges are parallel to edge *AB*?

b. Which edges intersect edge *AB*?

c. Which edges are skew to edge *AB*?

Solution

a. Edge *EF*, edge *CD* and edge *GH*.

b. Edge *AE*, edge *AD*, edge *BC* and edge *BF*.

c. Edge *EH*, edge *DH*, edge *FG* and edge *CG*.

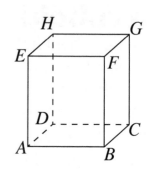

Practice 8.3

1. **Think of some real-life examples to illustrate the three potential positional relationships between two straight lines: intersecting, parallel and skew.**

2. **In the cuboid *ABCD-EFGH*, what is the maximum number of common points between any two edges? If there is no common point between two edges, does that mean they must be skew?**

3. **If you regard the pillars and roof of the building in this picture as straight lines, indicated by the red and green lines, what is the positional relationship between the two red lines? What about the red lines and the green line?**

4. **Look at the cupboard shown in the picture. Describe the positional relationships between the pole and the intersection of each face of the cuboid.**

8.4 Understanding the relationships between the edges and planes of a cuboid

Look at the diagram of cuboid *ABCD-EFGH* on the right. Edge *EF* and face *BCGF*, edge *FG* and face *ABFE*, and edge *BF* and face *ABCD* all give the image of a straight line, perpendicular to a plane.

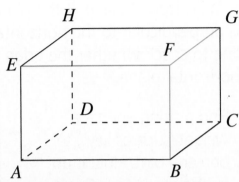

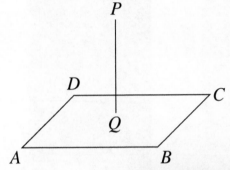

The straight line *PQ* is perpendicular to the plane *ABCD*. This is written as: line *PQ* ⊥ plane *ABCD*. It is read as: line *PQ* is perpendicular to plane *ABCD*.

If we regard the base of the monument or rocket launcher as a plane, and the monument or rocket as a straight line, they give the idea of a straight line perpendicular to a plane.

In a classroom, the wall at the front is perpendicular to the ceiling and the floor is perpendicular to the wall at the side.

? **Problem**

How can we check whether a straight line is perpendicular to a plane?

We can use a plumb line.

It is possible to use a plumb line to check whether a line is perpendicular to a horizontal plane. If the plumb line is parallel to the line, then the line is perpendicular to the horizontal plane. In this way, we can use a plumb line to check whether the edge of a blackboard is perpendicular to a horizontal plane.

Find a string and tie a weight (such as keys) to one end of it. Hold it up by the other end. This is a plumb line, a tool used since ancient times to determine a vertical line. Workers on construction sites often use plumb lines to check whether corners are perpendicular to the ground.

If a line is perpendicular to the wall, can we use a plumb line to check it?

No, but we can use a set square to check it.

Use a set square to check whether a line is perpendicular to a wall. Hold the set square with one of its perpendicular edges against the wall and the other perpendicular edge along the line you want to check. If the line is exactly along the other side of the right angle (flush with it), then the line is perpendicular to the wall.

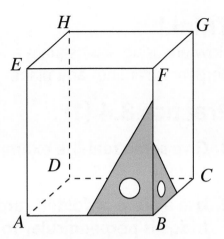

In the cuboid *ABCD-EFGH*, ∠*ABF* and ∠*CBF* are right angles, and they are like two set squares, each with a right-angled edge perpendicular to plane *ABCD*. Edge *AB* intersects edge *BC*, and the other side of the right angle is flush with edge BF, thus indicating that edge *BF* ⊥ plane *ABCD*.

We can also use folded card to check whether the line is perpendicular to the plane.

Fold a rectangular piece of card in half and then open it up to form an angle. It is shaped like the hinges of doors and windows. If the folded card stands upright on the table, we can see that the crease is perpendicular to the table.

Use the folded card to check whether a line is perpendicular to the table. When the folded card is upright on the table, if the crease is flush against the line then the line is perpendicular to the table.

In the cuboid *ABCD-EFGH*, the position of the plane *ADHE* and the plane *ABFE* are similar to a piece of folded card standing upright on plane *ABCD*. This indicates that edge *AE* ⊥ plane *ABCD*.

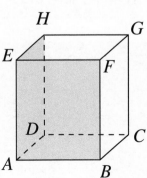

Think!
How are using a set square and using folded card to check for perpendicular lines and planes similar?

Practice 8.4 (1)

1. **Give some real-life examples where a line is perpendicular to a plane.**

2. **Use a piece of folded card to check whether the door of your fridge is perpendicular to the ground.**

3. **In the cuboid *ABCD-EFGH*:**
    a. Which edges are perpendicular to plane *ABCD*?
    b. Which planes are perpendicular to edge *EF*?
    c. How many planes are perpendicular to edge *AD*?

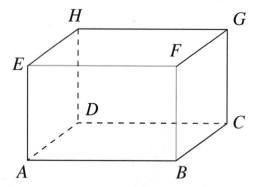

In the cuboid *ABCD-EFGH*, in the diagram above, we know that edge *EF* is perpendicular to plane *ABCD* and that edge *BF* is perpendicular to plane *ADHE*.

Line *PQ* is parallel to plane *ABCD*. This can be written as: line *PQ* ∥ plane *ABCD*. This is read as: line *PQ* is parallel to plane *ABCD*.

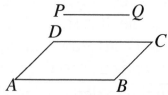

We know that the crossbars in this picture are parallel to the ground.

The plane of the classroom ceiling is parallel to the plane of the floor.

Problem

How can we check whether an edge is parallel to a plane?

We can use a plumb line to check.

We can use a plumb line to check whether the edge of the blackboard is parallel to the ground. We hold the plumb line from different points along the edge of the blackboard, letting the bottom of the plumb line just touch the ground. If the length of the plumb line from the blackboard to the ground is the same from two different points along the edge, then the edge of the blackboard is parallel to the ground.

We could also use a rectangular piece of paper.

We can use a rectangular piece of paper to check whether this cuboid desk lamp is parallel to the desktop. We put one edge of the rectangular piece of paper on the table. If its opposite edge is flush with the lamp, then the lamp is parallel to the table.

In the cuboid *ABCD-EFGH*, we can think of plane *ABFE* as a rectangular piece of paper. Edge *EF* is flush with plane *EFGH*, so we can say that edge *AB* ∥ plane *EFGH*.

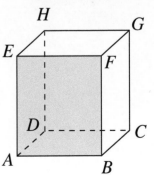

Think!

Are there any other geometric shapes that work the same as a rectangular piece of paper to check whether lines and planes are perpendicular?

> We could also use a parallelogram-shaped or trapezium-shaped piece of paper to check whether a line is parallel to a plane.

Example For the cuboid *ABCD-EFGH*:

a. If the edges that are parallel to plane *ABCD* were painted red, which edges would be painted red?

b. If the faces that are parallel to edge *BC* were painted blue, which faces would be painted blue?

Solution

a. Edge *EF*, edge *FG*, edge *GH* and edge *HE* would be painted red.

b. Plane *ADHE* and plane *EFGH* would be painted blue.

Practice 8.4 (2)

1. **Give some real-life examples of lines that are parallel to a plane.**

2. **In the cuboid in the diagram on the right:**
   a. Which edges are parallel to plane *ADHE*?
   b. Which planes are parallel to edge *EF*?

3. **Give a real-life example of where you could use a rectangular piece of paper to check whether an edge is parallel to a plane.**

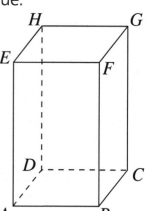

8.5 Understanding spatial relationships between two planes in a cuboid

In this geometric shape, we know that face *EFGH*, face *ABFE* and face *BCGF* are on the cuboid *ABCD-EFGH*. We know that any two of these faces are mutually perpendicular.

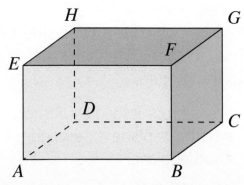

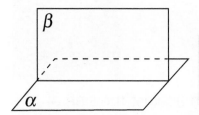

Plane α is perpendicular to plane β. This can be written as: plane $\alpha \perp$ plane β. This is read as: plane α is perpendicular to plane β.

The adjacent faces of the chalk boxes are mutually perpendicular.

The top face of the lorry is perpendicular to its four side faces.

If any two faces of the wall, the ceiling and the floor of the classroom are adjacent, they will be mutually perpendicular.

? Problem

How can you check that one plane is perpendicular to another?

Can we use a plumb line?

We can use a plumb line to check whether the side of a desk is perpendicular to the ground. If the plumb line is flush with the side of the desk, then the side of the desk is perpendicular to the ground.

Workers on construction sites often use plumb lines to check whether a wall is perpendicular to the ground.

We can use folded card to check whether a plane is perpendicular to another plane.

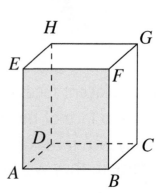

We can use folded card to check whether a shelf partition is perpendicular to the side of the shelf. Stand the folded card upright on the shelf, and if the line made by folding sits flush against the side of the shelf, then the shelf partition is perpendicular to the side of shelf.

In the cuboid *ABCD-EFGH*, we can think of plane *ADHE* and plane *ABFE* as folded card standing upright on plane *ABCD*. Line *AE* is like the line made by folding, and since it stands flush against plane *ABCD*, we can say that plane *ADHE* ⊥ plane *ABCD*.

Think!

Can we use a set square to check whether a plane is perpendicular to another plane?

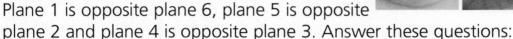

Example We can think of the dice in the picture as a cube. Its planes are named according to the number of dots on them. Plane 1 is opposite plane 6, plane 5 is opposite plane 2 and plane 4 is opposite plane 3. Answer these questions:

a. Which planes are perpendicular to plane 1?

b. Which planes are perpendicular to plane 4?

c. How many of these six planes are perpendicular to each other?

Solution

a. Plane 2, plane 3, plane 4 and plane 5 are all perpendicular to plane 1.

b. Plane 1, plane 2, plane 5, and plane 6 are all perpendicular to plane 4.

c. Of these six planes, 12 pairs of planes are perpendicular to each other.

Practice 8.5 (1)

1. **Give some real-life examples of where a plane is perpendicular to a plane.**

2. **Use folded card to check that whatever the position of the classroom door, it is always perpendicular to the ground.**

3. **For the cuboid $ABCD$-$EFGH$, find all planes that are perpendicular to plane $DCGH$.**

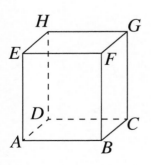

In the cuboid *JKLM-NOPQ* on the right, we know that plane *JKLM* is parallel to plane *NOPQ*, plane *KLPO* is parallel to plane *JMQN* and plane *JKON* is parallel to plane *MLPQ*.

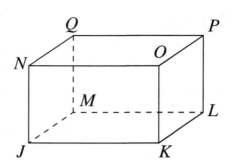

Plane α is parallel to plane β. This can be written as plane $\alpha \parallel$ plane β. This is read as: plane α is parallel to plane β.

The platform and springboard of a diving board are parallel to the surface of the water. We can guess that one plane is parallel to another plane from the picture.

The top shelf of the bookshelf and the bottom shelf of the bookshelf, the two side panels of the bookshelf, and the partitions in the filing cabinet are parallel to each other.

Of the wall, floor and ceiling of a classroom, the ceiling and the floor, the front wall and the back wall, and the left wall and the right wall are parallel to each other.

? Problem

How can we check whether a plane is parallel to another plane?

Can we use a rectangular piece of paper to check?

Can we use other shapes that are not rectangular?

We can use a rectangular piece of paper to check whether two pieces of cardboard are parallel to each other. We put the piece of paper at two points between the two pieces of cardboard. Each piece of paper should have one of its sides against one piece of cardboard and the opposite side against another. If this works well and both sides of the paper are flush against the two pieces of cardboard, then they are parallel to each other.

In the cuboid *ABCD-EFGH*, we can regard plane *ABFE* and plane *BCGF* as rectangular pieces of paper. Each of them has one edge flush against plane *ABCD* and the opposite edge against plane *EFGH*, so we can say that plane *ABCD* ∥ plane *EFGH*.

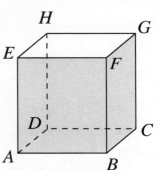

⟋ Practice 8.5 (2)

1. Give some real-life examples of where a plane is parallel to a plane.

2. a. For the cuboid *ABCD-EFGH*, write the planes that are parallel to plane *HGCD*.

b. Of the six planes in this cuboid, how many planes are parallel to each other?

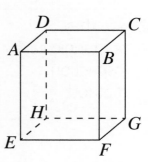

📖 Unit summary

In this unit you have looked at cuboids from two viewpoints. First, you explored their basic physical properties; then you examined positional relationships between their basic elements. When you are learning, you should make the most of basic properties of cuboids and their various shapes to help your understanding of various relationships between a cuboid's edges and planes. At the same time, you should use what you have learned to understand real-life objects.

The three properties of edges and planes
1. _____
2. _____
3. _____

Constructing a diagram of a cube

The relationship between edges and planes:
1. Are they parallel? Inspection method:

_____

2. Are they perpendicular? Inspection method:

_____

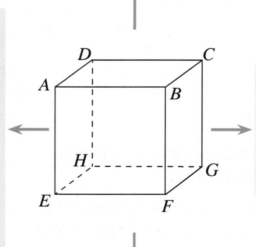

The relationship between edges and edges:
1. _____
2. _____
3. _____

The relationship between planes and planes:
1. Are they parallel? Inspection method: _____
2. Are they perpendicular? Inspection method: _____

Investigation activity: The quantitative relationship between the number of edges, the number of vertices and the number of faces of a cuboid

We know that a triangle has three edges and three vertices. A quadrilateral has four edges and four vertices. If we call the enclosed area surrounded by an edge a face, then triangles and quadrilaterals have only one face. Have you thought about the relationships between the numbers of edges, vertices and faces a shape has?

1. Write the numbers in the table.

	Triangle	Quadrilateral	Pentagon	Hexagon
Number of vertices (V)		4		
Number of edges (E)			5	
Number of faces (F)	1			1
$V - E + F$				

What conclusions can you draw from the table above? Does this conclusion hold true for other plane shapes?

2. Of the shapes below, only the first is a true cuboid. The others are all cuboids with a vertex missing. Count the edges, faces and vertices, and then write the numbers in the table on the next page.

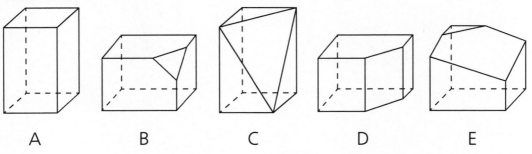

A   B   C   D   E

	A	B	C	D	E
Number of vertices (V)					
Number of edges (E)					
Number of faces (F)					
$V - E + F$					

What conclusions can you draw from the table above?

Extra reading material: The artist M. C. Escher

This unit begins with a picture of a faulty 'cuboid' (right). This frame doesn't exist in real life, but this picture is a work of art. M. C. Escher produced this kind of art.

M. C. Escher (Maurits Cornelis Escher, 1898–1972) was born in The Netherlands. His father, a hydraulic engineer, had assumed that Escher would follow him into the construction business. But he was not a good student. His poor grades and his preference for painting and design eventually led to a career in graphic art. By the time of his death in 1972, Escher had created hundreds of sketches, lithographs and wood engravings, leaving a rich cultural legacy for humanity.

Escher's works of art are unique and very popular across the world. Many works were based on the paradox of illusion and double meaning. He was like a magician, who presented charismatic 'impossible worlds'. To people's three-dimensional way of seeing, Escher's creations seem to be perfect as a partial view, but as a whole, the absurd and the real are unified perfectly.

Mathematicians, crystallographers and physicists showed great interest in Escher's work. Mathematicians praised him enthusiastically because they felt mathematical principles and ideas were well visualised in Escher's work. Escher's work involves many branches of maths; however, other than learning at school, this Dutch artist didn't have any formal training in mathematics, so this was particularly impressive.

In a recreation of the picture 'Waterfall' (right), from one point of view, water flows downwards from the top, but in the overall point of view, it flows upwards from bottom to top, making the mill wheels turn continuously like a perpetual motion machine. Is this possible, or is it absurd?

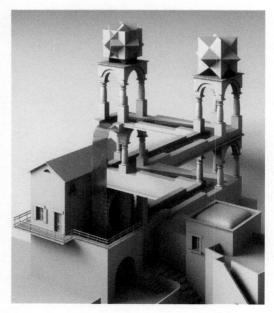